Devos for Brave Girls

Devos for Brave Girls

Katrina Cassel

Tyndale House Publishers
Carol Stream, Illinois

Visit Tyndale online at tyndale.com.

Visit Tyndale's website for kids at tyndale.com/kids.

TYNDALE is a registered trademark of Tyndale House Ministries. The Tyndale Kids logo is a trademark of Tyndale House Ministries.

Devos for Brave Girls

Adapted from *The One Year Devotions for Girls Starring Women of the Bible*, *ISBN 978-1-4143-3874-3* by Tyndale House Publishers, Inc., copyright © 2011 by Katrina Cassel. All rights reserved.

Cover background photograph of stars by Greg Jeanneau on Unsplash.

Designed by Lindsey Bergsma

For manufacturing information regarding this product, please call 1-855-277-9400.

For information about special discounts for bulk purchases, please contact Tyndale House Publishers at csresponse@tyndale.com, or call 1-855-277-9400.

ISBN 978-1-4964-5112-5

Printed in the United States of America

27 26 25 24 23 22 21
7   6   5   4   3   2   1

Created in God's Image

Read the beginning of Eve's story in Genesis 1:1-31.

*E*ve: the first woman. Made in the image of God. What exactly does that mean? It means that Eve was created as a reflection of God's glory. She had the ability to love, to be faithful, to show kindness, and to do many of the other things God does. It doesn't mean she physically resembled God, although God did design her and create her in a way that he said was very good (Genesis 1:31).

Many times people overlook how special Eve was as one of God's first creations, but God had a special plan for her. She was the first woman and the first mother. When God created Adam and Eve, he told them to have children and to fill the earth with people all created in his image. What an important job!

God gave Eve all she needed to fulfill his plan for her. And God has given you all you need to fulfill the wonderful plan he has for you. You may not know yet what you'll do in your adult life, but be assured, God has something special for you—then and now. You have been individually designed and specially made by God. There is no one on earth who has your same combination of looks, personality, talents, and abilities. Ephesians 2:10 says, "We are God's handiwork, created in Christ Jesus to do good works, which God prepared in advance for us to do" (NIV). God already knows his plan for you and created you to be just who you need to be in order to live out that plan. So determine now that you will go ahead and bravely be what God created you to be—a talented, still growing, still maturing young woman made to reflect God's glory.

Pray: Thank God for creating you and making your talents part of his plan for you.

> God created human beings in his own image. In the image of God he created them; male and female he created them.
> GENESIS 1:27

Making the Right Choice

Read about Eve's choice in Genesis 3:1-24.

God said, "You can have it all but this one thing."

Satan, speaking through the serpent, said, "God just doesn't want you to have something good."

Eve made the wrong choice to eat from the tree that God said not to eat from, and because of that one choice, sin entered the world. God could have put up an electric fence or a Do Not Touch sign, but he wanted Adam and Eve to choose obedience.

What could Eve have done differently when the serpent came along? She might have asked God about what the serpent said. What would have happened if Eve had said to the serpent, "Let me ask God about this when I talk with him in a little while"? Would the serpent have left and returned later to try again? Would it just have made up more lies that sounded true? We'll never know what might have happened. Eve made her choice, and the result is that we are all born with the tendency to disobey God.

You may not be visited by a serpent, but you will still be tempted to sin and face the decision every day whether to do what God says is right. But with every temptation, God will give you a way out. Ask God to give you the courage to obey his rules, and trust him to give you the rich and satisfying life he promises.

Pray: Ask the Holy Spirit to guide you and help you make right choices.

The instructions of the LORD are perfect, reviving the soul. The decrees of the LORD are trustworthy, making wise the simple.
PSALM 19:7

Quiz Time

*I*n the first devotion, we talked about the talents that God has given each of us. Not sure of your talent? Take the quiz below.

1. It's party time. What do you do?
   A. Design posters and decorations
   B. Teach everyone some cool new games
   C. Choose the music
   D. Make sure everyone is having fun
   E. Organize people to get jobs done
   F. Figure out how to set up cool disco lights
   G. Write a catchy invitation to get everyone to attend
   H. Figure out the party cost and make sure there is enough money
   I. Prepare the food

2. It's time to plan the family vacation. What do you want to do?
   A. Sketch scenery
   B. Horseback ride, ski, or surf
   C. Find a quiet place to play your guitar
   D. Meet new people
   E. Tour the White House or Senate
   F. Explore the Museum of Science and Technology
   G. Visit the home of a famous author
   H. Plan the route
   I. Help make your rustic cabin more like home

3. Which school elective would you choose?
   A. Art
   B. Physical education or cheerleading
   C. Chorus or drama
   D. Mentoring program (being a good role model)
   E. Speech
   F. Computer lab
   G. School newspaper or yearbook
   H. Math team
   I. Home economics (cooking, sewing, etc.)

4. What do you see yourself doing in fifteen years?
   A. Working in an art studio
   B. Coaching basketball
   C. Teaching music and drama at a high school
   D. Counseling people

E. Running a business or being mayor of my town
F. Working in a lab or teaching science
G. Writing mysteries or poetry
H. Working as an accountant or math teacher
I. Being an interior decorator or cake decorator

How many of each letter did you circle?

A ___ B ___ C ___ D ___ E ___ F ___ G ___ H ___ I ___

It's okay if you circled several different letters. You are still exploring all your talents and deciding what you like the most.

Mostly:
A: You have an eye for art. Whether it's drawing, ceramics, or water-color, your artistic ability shines through.
B: You have good coordination. Sports and physical activities come easily for you.
C: You have an ear for music or a flair for the dramatic. Expressing yourself in music or words is important to you.
D: You have a way with people. Whether it's classmates, children, or older adults, you relate to people and understand their feelings.
E: You have leadership ability. You can get people organized and motivated to work.
F: You have a good understanding of science and technology. New gadgets and concepts fascinate you.
G: You have a way with words. Whether it's reading or writing, you love the way words come together to form poems, stories, and ideas.
H: You reason and make good deductions. You are gifted with numbers and see the patterns in the world others might miss.
I: You like to cook, sew, and do other domestic things. You may design costumes, decorate cakes, or cook for a living.

Waiting for God

Read about God's promise to Sarah in Genesis 17:15-19.

God promised Abraham and Sarah that their family would be like the stars in the sky—it would be so big they wouldn't be able to count everyone. The problem with that? They didn't have any children. So there was no chance of grandchildren, let alone future generations.

Sarah knew that God had made a promise to Abraham and to her. But she didn't know how he would keep it. She knew that this promise was from the same God who created the world, the moon, sun, and stars, and all the animals and people. Certainly the God who did all this could cause Sarah to have a child, even in her old age. But it still seemed impossible.

Waiting for God to work isn't always easy, but it's the best thing. Running ahead of God or taking matters into your own hands often makes a mess of things. That doesn't mean God won't give you the wisdom and strength to handle some situations on your own. He will. He promises wisdom to those who ask (James 1:5). He will give you peace in your heart about choices you've made when they are the right ones. If you don't feel peace about a decision, it may not be the best choice or the right timing. If God says wait, then wait.

Pray: Tell God that you will trust his promises during times of waiting.

> They that wait upon the LORD shall renew their strength; they shall mount up with wings as eagles; they shall run, and not be weary; and they shall walk, and not faint.
> ISAIAH 40:31, KJV

God Hears

Read about God meeting Hagar in the desert in Genesis 16:1-15.

Hagar's story is intertwined with Sarah's. You'll remember God promised that Abraham and Sarah would start a great nation, but years passed, and they still had no children. Sarah came up with her own plan. She told Abraham to have a child with her servant, Hagar. So Abraham did what Sarah asked, and Hagar became pregnant.

Sarah had wanted to have a child for years, but it was Hagar who was pregnant. Hagar began to tease Sarah. Sarah became jealous and angry. No one was winning. Abraham told Sarah to handle it however she wanted, and Sarah mistreated Hagar. The situation was so bad that Hagar fled to the desert to escape Sarah.

In the desert, Hagar was probably lonely, frightened, and not sure what would happen to her. Then an angel came to Hagar and told her to return to Sarah and submit to her. The angel promised Hagar that God would handle the situation. Thankfully God is a God who can fix problems. The angel told Hagar she would have a son and that she should call him Ishmael, which means "God hears." God promised to make Ishmael's descendants into a great nation.

If you are facing difficulties today, God does hear your prayers for help. He will work out your problems just as he worked out Hagar's. God didn't leave Hagar alone in her despair, and he doesn't leave you alone either. Spend time talking to the God who hears and bravely trust him to take care of you.

Pray: Tell God your problems and be confident that he will hear you and help you.

> The angel of the LORD found Hagar beside a spring of water in the wilderness, along the road to Shur.
>
> GENESIS 16:7

Puzzle Page

Sarah had to wait a long time for her prayers to be answered. What did the psalmist say about waiting? Solve the Balloon Puzzle to find out.

Directions: Each balloon has both a scrambled word and a number in it. There are also numbers next to the blank spots in the verse. Look at the number next to each blank. Find the balloon with the same number. Unscramble the word in that balloon, and write it in the blank. Check your answers at the bottom.

1. _____ 2. _____ for the 3. _____. Be 4. _____

and 5. _____. Yes, 1. _____ 2. _____ for the

3. _____.

What two things does this verse tell you to do while you wait? How can you do them?

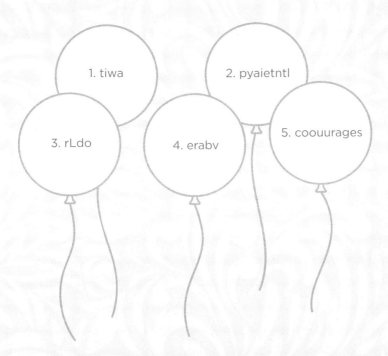

1. tiwa

2. pyaietntl

3. rLdo

4. erabv

5. coouurages

7

God Keeps His Promises

Read about the birth of Sarah's son, Isaac, in Genesis 21:1-7.

Many years passed between when God first promised to make Abraham and Sarah a great nation and when Sarah actually gave birth to their son, Isaac. During the wait, Sarah had a lot of time to worry, doubt, fear, plan, pray, and trust.

But eventually, the years of waiting were over. God had heard Sarah's prayers and answered. Now, at ninety years old, Sarah had her long-promised baby. Why didn't God answer Sarah's prayer years earlier and give her a child while she was young? Or even a whole houseful of children? The Bible doesn't give a reason, but it does say God is in control of all things. He could have filled Abraham and Sarah's house with a dozen children right away. For some reason, God chose to make Sarah wait for the desire of her heart.

God sees the whole picture of our lives, while we see only a section at a time. God knew how Abraham's and Sarah's lives would play out, and he decided how many children they would have and when. We don't always know the "whys" of God's answers, but we can trust that he always keeps his promises.

Do things in your life seem confusing right now? Are there situations that make you wonder if God is listening and if he really cares? The God of Sarah and Abraham is the same God who is watching over you. He has given you his message in his Word, the Bible. He has promises for you in the Bible that are as true today as they were when the Bible was first written. You can courageously claim them for your own and believe them as though they were written just for you.

Pray: Thank God for being faithful to you and always keeping his promises.

> "For the mountains may move and the hills disappear, but even then my faithful love for you will remain. My covenant of blessing will never be broken," says the LORD, who has mercy on you.
> ISAIAH 54:10

Don't Look Back

Read the end of Lot's wife's story in Genesis 19:15-26.

L ot and his family lived in Sodom. The city was filled with people living in very ungodly ways. The people were so wicked that God was going to destroy the city along with the city of Gomorrah.

Abraham begged God to save his nephew Lot and Lot's family. God sent angels to warn Lot that the city would be destroyed. He and his family needed to leave. Lot led his wife and his two daughters reluctantly out of the city. Even though the city was going to be destroyed, Lot's family didn't want to leave. They owned many things, and it was hard to leave them behind. But they believed God would destroy the city.

The angels told Lot and his family to hurry, not to stop until they got to the next village, and not to look back. But Mrs. Lot didn't want to leave her old life behind, and she made a big mistake. She looked back, and God turned her into a pillar of salt.

Jesus uses Lot's wife as an illustration to warn people about the end times: "Remember what happened to Lot's wife! If you cling to your life, you will lose it, and if you let your life go, you will save it" (Luke 17:32-33). Jesus warns people to leave their old sinful ways behind while there is still time.

It's important to decide now to follow Jesus. Once you do, don't be like Lot's wife. Instead, look ahead to the hope and purpose you have in God.

Pray: Ask God for the courage to leave behind anything that distracts you from following him.

> Everyone who has given up houses or brothers or sisters or father or mother or children or property, for my sake, will receive a hundred times as much in return and will inherit eternal life.
> MATTHEW 19:29

Puzzle Page

*M*rs. Lot turned backward toward the life she left behind instead of courageously trusting God with her future. The book of Proverbs has some good advice for us. Use the Box Code below to help you decode the verse.

	♦	●	♥	✖	✚
✪	A	C	D	E	G
◆	H	I	K	L	M
❖	N	O	P	R	S
♣	T	U	W	Y	Q

_____ _____ ____ L<small>ORD</small>
♣♦ ❖✖ ♣● ❖✚ ♣♦ ◆● ❖❖ ♣♦ ◆♦ ✪✖

with _____ your _____; _____ not
✪♦ ◆✖ ◆✖   ◆✖ ✪✖ ✪♦ ❖✖ ♣♦   ✪♥ ❖●

_____ on_____ _____
✪♥ ✪✖ ❖♥ ✪✖ ❖♦ ✪♥   ♣✖ ❖● ♣● ❖✖   ❖● ♣♥ ❖❖

understanding. _____ _____ _____
❖✚ ✪✖ ✪✖ ◆♥ ◆♦ ◆● ❖✚ ♣♥ ◆● ◆✖ ◆✖

in all _____ _____, and _____
♣✖ ❖● ♣● ✪♥ ❖●   ◆♦ ✪✖ ♣♥ ◆● ◆✖ ◆✖

_____
❖✚ ◆♦ ❖● ♣♥ ♣✖ ❖● ♣● ♣♥ ◆♦ ◆● ✪● ◆♦

_____ to _____.
❖♥ ✪♦ ♣♦ ◆♦   ♣♦ ✪♦ ◆♥ ✪✖

When you trust God, he will show you which choices are the right ones. You will know which path to take. How can you trust God today?

Go the Extra Mile

Read about Rebekah's experience at the well in Genesis 24:15-20.

Have you heard the expression "Go the extra mile"? Going the extra mile means you do a little more than is expected or required. Most people probably don't realize that the expression is actually based on a verse from Jesus' Sermon on the Mount, found in Matthew 5.

Jesus also told the story of the Good Samaritan, someone who literally went the extra mile. Not only did he stop and patch up a wounded stranger, but he also took him to an inn and even paid for his care. Sometimes it's easier to look the other way when someone needs help. That's what the others did in the story of the Good Samaritan. But it was the Samaritan who made the best choice when he not only stopped to help but also went the extra mile.

Rebekah went the extra mile too. She granted Eliezer's request for a drink, and then she also watered his camels. This isn't like giving a dog water, where you pour a few cups of water in the bowl twice a day and you're done. A camel can drink up to twenty-five gallons of water after a long journey, and Eliezer's ten camels had just made a five-hundred-mile trek. That meant Rebekah lifted pitcher after heavy pitcher of water out of the well. She didn't know Eliezer, and the camels weren't her family's camels, but she went the extra mile to do what she felt she should do.

Sometimes it's easier to look the other way or just do what's required, but it's much better to be like Rebekah and go the extra mile.

Pray: Ask God to show you how you can go the extra mile today—no matter who asks.

> If a soldier demands that you carry his gear for a mile, carry it two miles. Give to those who ask, and don't turn away from those who want to borrow.
>
> **MATTHEW 5:41-42**

A Journey of Faith

Read about Rebekah's decision to trust God with her future in Genesis 24:50-61.

After his camels were cared for, Eliezer asked Rebekah whose daughter she was. She identified herself to him. Eliezer asked her if there was room for him at her house. She responded that they not only had room for him, but they had straw and fodder for the camels, too.

Eliezer went to Rebekah's home. He told her family that he had come to find a wife for Abraham and Sarah's son, Isaac, and he gave gifts to the family members. It was agreed that Rebekah would become Isaac's wife. Eliezer spent the night with the family, and the next day he was anxious to begin the long journey back home.

Rebekah's family asked that he give the family ten days before he took Rebekah home to marry Isaac, but Eliezer wanted to leave immediately. The family said it was up to Rebekah. They called her in and asked her if she would go with Eliezer right away.

Rebekah said, "I will go." She packed up and began a journey of faith to see the man she was going to marry—a man she had never met.

Her family had decided that her marriage to Isaac was a good plan, but Rebekah had to agree. She agreed not only to marry Isaac but also to leave the very next morning on a long trip through the desert. She took only her nurse, Deborah, with her. Rebekah packed and bade her family farewell, knowing she would probably never see them again. Then she went with Eliezer.

It may have been scary for Rebekah to leave everything behind for a man she'd never met, but she trusted that this was the path God had for her. If Rebekah had not been willing to step out in faith, she would have missed all God had planned for her.

Pray: Ask God to help you trust him with your future.

> Trust in the LORD with all your heart; do not depend on your own understanding. Seek his will in all you do, and he will show you which path to take.
> PROVERBS 3:5-6

Puzzle Page

W̲e've been learning about Rebekah's faith in God. What does the Bible say about faith? Use the Box Code below to help you decode the verse.

	◆	●	♥	✖	✚
✪	A	B	E	F	G
✦	H	I	L	N	O
❖	S	T	V	W	Y

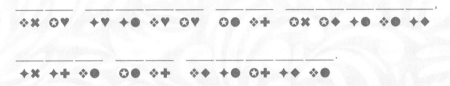

❖✖ ✪♥   ✦♥ ✦● ❖♥ ✪♥   ●● ❖✚   ✪✖ ✪◆ ✦● ❖● ✦◆ ,

✦✖ ✦✚ ❖●   ✪● ❖✚   ❖◆ ✦● ✪✚ ✦◆ ❖● .

Is this verse true about Rebekah? Why or why not? How can this verse apply to you?

Overcoming Obstacles

Read about God's promise to always love and help you in Romans 8:35-39.

As you read about women in the Bible, are you noticing some common themes? One thing that stands out is that all the women had problems, some of them heartbreaking or with no obvious solution. But each woman overcame her obstacles with God's help. Many times God intervened directly to solve the problem.

Often waiting was part of the woman's life. Sarah waited years to have a child. She was ninety by the time it happened. Rebekah also waited, disappointed year after year when no child came. Many of the women faced changes. Eve left her familiar garden home. Sarah moved twice. Hagar despaired in the desert. Rebekah traveled five hundred miles to be married.

Whether the situation involved an inability to have children, a long journey, a new world, bitterness, or feeling unloved, God was at work through it. We remember the women for the problems they overcame with God's help.

You may be facing problems in your life. Perhaps your parents are getting divorced, or one of them is getting remarried and adding step-siblings to the family. Maybe you have a disease your friends don't understand. Maybe school is hard for you, or maybe you are dealing with a bully. Maybe your sister is mean to you, or your best friend just decided she wanted to be best friends with someone else. These things are part of your life for now, but the ending is not yet written.

Stay close to God and ask him to help you be brave. He will give you solutions and help just as he did for the women of the Bible. He knows and cares about you just as much as he did those women.

Pray: Thank God that nothing can separate you from his love.

No, despite all these things, overwhelming victory is ours through Christ, who loved us.
ROMANS 8:37

Choosing to Do Right

Read about Shiphrah and Puah's courageous choice in Exodus 1:15-21.

Rebekah's grandson, Joseph, ended up in Egypt, where God warned him of a coming famine, and the pharaoh, or king, put him in charge of storing up food ahead of time.

Many years passed. Joseph and all his brothers were dead. His family, known as the Israelites, had grown immensely. Now there were so many Israelites in Egypt that the new pharaoh, who didn't know Joseph's story, was afraid the Israelites would fight against them and take over the land.

To keep this from happening, he made the Israelites slaves. That didn't keep them from becoming greater in number, though. So Pharaoh ordered the midwives (women who helped deliver babies) to kill all the baby boys born to the Hebrew (Israelite) women.

Shiphrah and Puah were two brave midwives who knew they couldn't follow that order. Instead, they disobeyed Pharaoh and risked severe punishment in order to spare the innocent baby boys. God saw that Shiphrah and Puah had made a choice to honor him, and he blessed them for it. He kept them safe from Pharaoh, and he gave them families of their own.

You will face many choices in life. Some are easy; some aren't. And sometimes the choice comes down to whether you will do what's right or take the easy way out. You may think you will always choose right, but sometimes the choice is difficult. You might feel like you are the only one trying to please God and trying to stand firm.

When you are faced with a difficult choice, trust God's promise for you in 1 Corinthians 15:58: "Be strong and immovable. Always work enthusiastically for the Lord, for you know that nothing you do for the Lord is ever useless."

Pray: Ask God to make you brave and help you to obey him when faced with a tough choice.

> Now, Israel, what does the LORD your God require of you?
> He requires only that you fear the LORD your God, and live in
> a way that pleases him, and love him and serve him with all
> your heart and soul.
> DEUTERONOMY 10:12

Puzzle Page

We learned that Shiphrah and Puah risked their lives in order to do what was right. If you follow God, he will give you the power to obey him. Solve the puzzle below and reflect on God's promise.

Directions: The words in the word bank fit into the boxes below. The best way to solve these puzzles is to start with the longest words first. Then, if you have many short words with the same number of letters left, you can fill them in based on which word makes sense in each box. Give it a try.

| For | to | you | pleases | power | God | the |
| giving | do | you | desire | working | what | him |

___ ___ ___   ___ ___ ___   is   ___ ___ ___ ___ ___ ___ ___   in

___ ___ ___ ,   ___ ___ ___ ___ ___ ___   ___ ___ ___   the

___ ___ ___ ___ ___ ___ ___   and   ___ ___ ___   ___ ___ ___ ___ ___

___ ___ ___   ___ ___ ___   ___ ___ ___ ___ ___

___ ___ ___ ___ ___ ___ ___ ___   ___ ___ ___ ___ .

Sacrificial Faith

Read about the incredible faith of Moses' mother in Exodus 2:1-10.

*J*ochebed was a woman with a problem. Her son was in danger, and she needed to do something about it.

When Pharaoh's plan to have the midwives kill all the Hebrew baby boys didn't work, he ordered the baby boys to be thrown into the river.

During this time, Jochebed gave birth to Moses. She knew from the beginning that he was a special child and was destined to do great things. She hid him for three months, but then it became too difficult to hide him. If you have a baby sibling or you babysit, you understand this. Babies don't like to lie quietly doing nothing. So Jochebed made a special basket for Moses, waterproofed it, and placed it in the reeds along the edge of the Nile River.

You might know what happened next. The pharaoh's own daughter found Moses and realized he was a Hebrew baby. She wanted to raise him as her own but needed someone to care for him until he was old enough to live at the palace. Moses' sister, Miriam, who was watching nearby, offered to get her mother to help. So Moses ended up staying with his own family during his earliest years.

Jochebed didn't know what would happen when she put Moses in the river, but she had faith that God was in control of all things. It was that faith that allowed her to keep Moses safe even if it meant giving him up. It's never easy to make sacrifices, especially when we aren't sure of the outcome, but Jochebed's faith in God was strong enough for her to surrender her son to God's work.

God may ask you to sacrifice something in order to fulfill his plans for you. No matter what that looks like, the important thing to remember is that when God asks you to give something up, he always has something much better in mind for you.

Pray: Ask God to strengthen your faith in him.

> It was by faith that Moses' parents hid him for three months when he was born. They saw that God had given them an unusual child, and they were not afraid to disobey the king's command.
> **HEBREWS 11:23**

God's Power on Display

Read the song Miriam and the Israelites sang to God after he rescued them from the Egyptians in Exodus 15:1-21.

*I*n her youth, Miriam was a devoted sister to Moses. In her adult years, Miriam took part in leading the people of Israel out of slavery alongside her brothers, Moses and Aaron. Miriam had already seen God work. First she witnessed God's care of baby Moses when the pharaoh's daughter found him and spared his life. Although she didn't see it, she knew that God spoke to Moses from a burning bush and told Moses he was chosen to lead God's people out of slavery.

Next Miriam heard of God's power when Aaron's staff turned into a snake in front of Pharaoh. This was followed by ten plagues sent by God to convince the pharaoh to let the Israelites go. Miriam watched the river turn into blood, frogs invade the land, dust turn into gnats, and flies swarm the region. She saw all the Egyptian livestock die, boils break out on the people, hail kill people and animals, locusts devour the crops, darkness cover the land for three days, and finally, the first-born children and animals die. Many of these things happened only to the Egyptians, not to the Hebrews.

Miriam witnessed God's miraculous power over and over. She realized that everything she was seeing was God at work. When the pharaoh agreed to free the slaves, Miriam was ready to step in and help her brothers lead the Israelites to the Promised Land.

We don't often get to witness miraculous acts of God like those Miriam saw. But we can see God work in many little ways around us. The book of Romans says that nature points to God (Romans 1:20). Think of the change of seasons: the heat of the sun, the falling leaves, and the arrival of snow show God's power. Look for God's power all around you today.

Pray: Praise God for all the ways—both big and small—that you have seen his power at work in your life.

> And Miriam sang this song: "Sing to the LORD, for he has triumphed gloriously; he has hurled both horse and rider into the sea."
> EXODUS 15:21

Quiz Time

*W*e've been learning how God helped Jochebed deal with her big problem. How well are you dealing with a problem in your life? Take the quiz below to find out.

1. Your best friend isn't talking to you. You see her look at you and then whisper to another girl. You
   A. have another friend ask her what is going on.
   B. ignore her. Whatever happened will blow over in a few days.
   C. call her after school and ask her if you did something to upset her.

2. Tryouts for the Easter musical are next week. You don't think you sing well enough to get a good role, but your grandma is coming for Easter and assumes you will be in the program. You don't want to disappoint her. You
   A. have your mom tell her that you aren't going to be in it.
   B. pretend to be sick the day of tryouts. Then you have an excuse for not being in the program.
   C. give it a try. Even if you don't get one of the big roles, you may get a small part, and you can do your best with it.

3. It's the night before science projects are due, and your real-life erupting volcano blows up! You
   A. have your dad write a note to the teacher explaining what happened.
   B. don't turn in a project. There's not enough time to redo it.
   C. take in your report and display board, complete with pictures of the aftermath of the eruption. The volcano worked!

How did you do?

Mostly:
A: You have other people solve your problems for you. It's okay to get assistance, but with God's help, you can work through some problems yourself.
B: You tend to avoid problems. But that doesn't make them go away! Sometimes it even makes them worse. Ask someone to brainstorm possible solutions with you, then choose the best one and act on it.
C: You try to solve your problems by seeing what needs to be done and doing it. You realize that things don't always turn out like you want, but it's still important to step out in faith and give it a try.

Leadership through Service

Read what Jesus has to say about serving others in Matthew 20:25-28.

One thing that set Miriam, Moses, and Aaron apart as leaders is that they served the people rather than expecting people to serve them. The trio journeyed among the people they were leading. They took part in the work and never asked others to do what they themselves weren't willing to do. They were hard workers. You wouldn't find them lounging in their tents while others waited on them. Serving others is a true mark of a leader but one you don't see often.

Jesus is our ultimate example of a leader who served others. He didn't come to earth as a king on a throne. He didn't demand special treatment because he is the Son of God. He worked alongside his earthly father in a carpenter shop. He spent time with the poor and the sick. He didn't live in a mansion or have riches. He traveled with only the clothes on his back. He took on himself the lowly task of washing his disciples' feet to illustrate that the person who wants to be great must be a servant to others.

Being able to give a speech to a large crowd isn't the mark of a true leader, and neither is making a grand entrance. Having a large group of followers doesn't make one a great leader, nor does being dressed better or owning more things than others.

Moses and Jesus are models of true leaders. If you want to be a great leader, fearlessly follow their examples. And look for leaders today who lead by serving others.

Pray: Ask God to help you serve others with a humble heart.

> Make me truly happy by agreeing wholeheartedly with each other, loving one another, and working together with one mind and purpose. Don't be selfish; don't try to impress others. Be humble, thinking of others as better than yourselves. Don't look out only for your own interests, but take an interest in others, too.
> **PHILIPPIANS 2:2-4**

Acting in Faith

Read about Rahab hiding the Israelite spies in Joshua 2:1-24.

*J*oshua and the people of Israel are on the doorstep to the Promised Land when we first meet Rahab in the Bible. Joshua sent two spies to check out the land of Jericho. The Israelites would have to conquer it to claim the Promised Land.

The spies went to Rahab's house. She lived in a house on the wall surrounding Jericho. The wall was wide enough on top for buildings and a road. Because Rahab entertained all sorts of men at her house, two unknown spies wouldn't be noticeable there. People were used to seeing men come and go. Rahab's house would give the spies a chance to look over the city and also study the walls, which they would have to get through to conquer Jericho.

Eventually, some men who lived in Jericho found out the Israelite spies were at Rahab's house and went to capture them. The men asked Rahab to turn the spies over to them. Rahab told them the spies had already left, and she urged them to hurry so they could catch up with the spies.

Rahab risked her life to save the spies. She'd hidden them under flax on her rooftop. If they had been found, she would have been punished, possibly by death.

Rahab made a faith choice. She told the spies that her people had heard what God did years before in parting the Red Sea and how the Israelites had defeated many nations. She declared that the Lord is God in heaven above and on earth below. Rahab chose the God of the Israelites over her pagan gods.

The spies promised to save Rahab as long as she left a scarlet cord hanging from the window through which they escaped. They told her that her family must also be in the house to be saved.

Rahab placed her faith in God and trusted the spies to keep their word. She did what they said, and when the walls of Jericho fell, she and her family were saved.

Pray: Thank God for the gift of his salvation.

> He saved us, not because of the righteous things we had done,
> but because of his mercy. He washed away our sins, giving us
> a new birth and new life through the Holy Spirit.
> TITUS 3:5

Puzzle Page

*D*ecode the Thermometer Puzzle below to read a verse that applies to each of us concerning God's grace.

Directions: Look at the thermometer. Each temperature has a corresponding letter. Look at the temperatures under the lines below. Above each line, write the letter that goes with the temperature. Check your answers below.

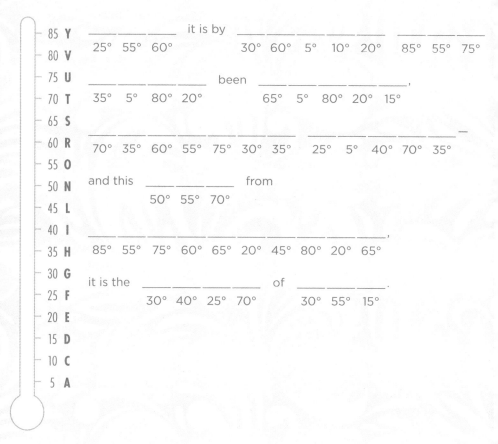

85 **Y**
80 **V**
75 **U**
70 **T**
65 **S**
60 **R**
55 **O**
50 **N**
45 **L**
40 **I**
35 **H**
30 **G**
25 **F**
20 **E**
15 **D**
10 **C**
5 **A**

___ ___ ___ it is by ___ ___ ___ ___ ___ ___ ___ ___
25° 55° 60°   30° 60° 5° 10° 20°   85° 55° 75°

___ ___ ___ ___ been ___ ___ ___ ___ ___ ,
35° 5° 80° 20°   65° 5° 80° 20° 15°

___ ___ ___ ___ ___ ___ ___ ___ ___ ___ ___ ___ —
70° 35° 60° 55° 75° 30° 35°   25° 5° 40° 70° 35°

and this ___ ___ ___ from
50° 55° 70°

___ ___ ___ ___ ___ ___ ___ ___ ___ ___ ,
85° 55° 75° 60° 65° 20° 45° 80° 20° 65°

it is the ___ ___ ___ ___ of ___ ___ ___ .
30° 40° 25° 70°   30° 55° 15°

No Turning Back

Read about God protecting Rahab and rewarding her faith in Joshua 6:22-25.

ahab made several choices, and once she did, there was no turning back. First she chose to let the spies into her house. She knew they weren't from Jericho. They dressed and talked differently from the men she saw every day. Then she chose to hide them and send those looking for them another way.

Rahab chose to believe God sent these men, and that God was going to destroy her city. And finally Rahab decided that she wouldn't be destroyed along with the others. She made the spies promise to spare her. Then she acted on faith and did exactly what they told her to do. She hung a scarlet cord out her window and gathered her family so they would be spared too.

Once Rahab did these things, there was no turning back. In fact, there was nowhere to turn back to. Her city was gone. How different Rahab was from Mrs. Lot, who didn't want to leave her home even though it was going to be destroyed. Mrs. Lot looked back and longed for all she had left behind. Not Rahab. She took the escape route the spies provided and lived among the Israelites from that time on. Mrs. Lot was one of a handful of godly people in all of Sodom, yet she is remembered for her tragic choice. Rahab had lived a sinful lifestyle before she met the Israelite spies, yet she chose to honor God and help his people, and she is known as a hero of faith.

Rahab made her choice, and she was all in. Do you share that same desire? Will you follow Jesus wholeheartedly?

Pray: Ask God to give you the courage to follow him with all your heart.

> Joshua spared Rahab the prostitute and her relatives who were with her in the house, because she had hidden the spies Joshua sent to Jericho. And she lives among the Israelites to this day.
> **JOSHUA 6:25**

God Raises Up a Rescuer

Read about Deborah's job as judge in Judges 4:1-5.

The book of Judges is full of stories of courage. It is also a sad book because of the Israelites' failure to obey God and trust him. When the Israelites went in and took the Promised Land, they didn't drive out all the enemies as God had commanded them.

Sometimes these enemies rose up and dominated the Israelites until God sent a leader—called a judge—to deliver them. Then there would be peace in the land, and the people would obey God.

After a while the people would start doing whatever they wanted and disobeying God again—and another nation would conquer them. They would again turn to God, and he would raise up another leader to deliver them. This happened over and over. It seemed the Israelites would never learn.

Out of this darkness and oppression, God raised up Deborah, a remarkable woman who shared many character traits with the other women you've read about in this book. She had faith like Sarah's. She had initiative just as Rebekah did. She had courage as Shiphrah and Puah did. She was creative like Jochebed. She had leadership abilities like Miriam's.

In fact, Deborah had everything God needed to rescue his people from the Canaanites—wisdom, courage, initiative, strength, and spiritual insight. Beyond that, Deborah had faith that God would give her the victory, and she didn't waver.

We can learn much from Deborah, who lived her life courageously and passionately as she charged headfirst into all God had planned for her.

Pray: Thank God that he uses faithful women to accomplish his purposes.

Deborah, the wife of Lappidoth, was a prophet who was judging Israel at that time. She would sit under the Palm of Deborah, between Ramah and Bethel in the hill country of Ephraim, and the Israelites would go to her for judgment.
JUDGES 4:4

Puzzle Page

*D*eborah had many gifts that God used to rescue the Israelites from their enemies. God has also given you gifts so you can serve others and accomplish good. Solve this Telephone Puzzle to see what the Bible says about your gifts.

Directions: This puzzle has two numbers under each blank. The first number matches one of the phone buttons. The second number tells you which letter on the button to write down. For instance, "9.3" means letter 3 on button 9. Check your answer below.

If ____ ____ ____ ____ ____ ____ ____ ____ is to
9.3 6.3 8.2 7.3   4.1 4.3 3.3 8.1

____ ____ ____ ____ ____ ____ ____ ____ ____
3.2 6.2 2.3 6.3 8.2 7.3 2.1 4.1 3.2

____ ____ ____ ____ ____ ____, be
6.3 8.1 4.2 3.2 7.3 7.4

____ ____ ____ ____ ____ ____ ____ ____ ____ ____ ____.
3.2 6.2 2.3 6.3 8.2 7.3 2.1 4.1 4.3 6.2 4.1

If it is ____ ____ ____ ____ ____ ____, ____ ____ ____ ____
4.1 4.3 8.3 4.3 6.2 4.1   4.1 4.3 8.3 3.2

____ ____ ____ ____ ____ ____ ____ ____ ____ ____. If ____ ____ ____
4.1 3.2 6.2 3.2 7.3 6.3 8.2 7.4 5.3 9.3   4.1 6.3 3.1

has ____ ____ ____ ____ ____ you leadership
4.1 4.3 8.3 3.2 6.2

____ ____ ____ ____ ____ ____ ____, take the responsibility
2.1 2.2 4.3 5.3 4.3 8.1 9.3

____ ____ ____ ____ ____ ____ ____ ____ ____. And if you have a
7.4 3.2 7.3 4.3 6.3 8.2 7.4 5.3 9.3

____ ____ ____ ____ for ____ ____ ____ ____ ____ ____ ____
4.1 4.3 3.3 8.1   7.4 4.2 6.3 9.1 4.3 6.2 4.1

____ ____ ____ ____ ____ ____ ____ ____ to
5.2 4.3 6.2 3.1 6.2 3.2 7.4 7.4

____ ____ ____ ____ ____ ____, do it ____ ____ ____ ____ ____ ____.
6.3 8.1 4.2 3.2 7.3 7.4   4.1 5.3 2.1 3.1 5.3 9.3

How can you live this verse today?

Phone buttons:
1	2 ABC	3 DEF
4 GHI	5 JKL	6 MNO
7 PQRS	8 TUV	9 WXYZ
*	0 OPER	#

A Courageous Woman

Read about Deborah leading the Israelite army into battle in Judges 4:6-24.

While Deborah was sitting under her palm tree counseling others, she sent for Barak. Deborah told him God wanted him to go into battle against Sisera and his nine hundred chariots of iron. She even told him how God was going to give him the victory.

How did Barak, the army general, respond? "I won't go unless you go with me." This might not have been such a strange request except that Barak was talking to a woman. In Bible times, women were not in the military. Yet Barak wasn't willing to go into battle without Deborah. He felt her presence would ensure their victory.

What did Deborah do? She agreed to go. No sitting under her tree counseling others while Barak went to fight. She would be right in the midst of the battle. Deborah wasn't afraid. She knew God was with her, and the victory was already sure. But because Barak wasn't willing to trust God and go into battle without her, Deborah prophesied that Sisera would fall to a woman. (She wasn't prophesying about herself, but about Jael, who killed Sisera in the end.)

Deborah had total faith in God, and that faith gave her courage. The Israelites didn't have chariots or fancy swords and shields, but they had the power of God. Can you imagine Deborah as she went into battle, the lone woman among ten thousand men? A courageous woman posted among the men in the woods on the mountainside, watching as God gave them the victory he had promised?

No wonder Deborah tells the story in song afterward. She had done something other women hadn't done. She'd displayed more courage than mighty Barak, and she'd done it by faith alone.

Pray: Tell God that you want to be brave for him.

> This is my command—be strong and courageous! Do not be afraid or discouraged. For the LORD your God is with you wherever you go.
> JOSHUA 1:9

When Everything Is Gone

Read about Naomi's family tragedy in Ruth 1:1-5.

*N*aomi and her husband, Elimelech, lived in Bethlehem. They were likely well-known and highly respected in this small Jewish town. Life was going well. Naomi gave birth to two boys, and the whole family loved and served God.

Then things fell apart. There was a famine, food was scarce, and Elimelech feared his family would die. He made the choice to move his family to Moab, where there was food.

Unfortunately, tragedy continued to strike Elimelech's family in Moab. First Elimelech himself died. Next Elimelech and Naomi's two sons, Mahlon and Kilion, married Moabite women—even though God's law said they should only marry other Israelites.

Sometime after this, both sons died. Again, we don't know how or why or even if they died at the same time. All the Bible tells us is that they died, and neither had a child.

Naomi, once well-loved and surrounded by friends and family in her own land, was now alone in a foreign country except for two Moabite daughters-in-law, grieving the loss of her husband and two sons. She didn't have any friends who shared her faith or worshiped her God. In fact, Naomi felt God himself had forsaken her.

Naomi was filled with grief and despair. Everything was gone. How she must have regretted the day her family left Bethlehem for Moab. But thankfully, this wasn't the end of the story for Naomi.

With God there is always hope. He knows all the problems that we face in this world, and he will be with you through whatever difficulties you experience. Trust his plans for you.

Pray: Thank God that nothing can stop him from accomplishing his good plans for your life.

> And we know that in all things God works for the good
> of those who love him, who have been called according to
> his purpose.
> ROMANS 8:28, NIV

Puzzle Page

$\mathcal{W}$ e will face hard times in our lives, just as Naomi did, but Jesus has comforting words for us. Fill in the puzzle to read Jesus' words.

Directions: The words in the word bank fit into the boxes below. The best way to solve these puzzles is to start with the longest words first. Then, if you have many short words with the same number of letters left, you can fill them in based on which word makes sense in each box. Give it a try.

trials	earth	overcome	have	will
many	take	Here	you	heart
sorrows	because	have	world	

___ ___ ___ ___ on ___ ___ ___ ___ ___ ___ ___ ___

___ ___ ___ ___ ___ ___ ___ ___ ___ ___ ___ ___ ___ ___

___ ___ ___ ___ ___ ___ ___ and ___ ___ ___ ___ ___ ___ ___ .

But ___ ___ ___ ___ ___ ___ ___ ___ ___ ,

___ ___ ___ ___ ___ ___ ___ I ___ ___ ___ ___

___ ___ ___ ___ ___ ___ ___ ___ the ___ ___ ___ ___ ___ .

Answer: Here on earth you will have many trials and sorrows. But take heart, because I have overcome the world (John 16:33).

28

Returning Home Empty

Read about Naomi's return to Bethlehem in Ruth 1:19-22.

*N*aomi left Bethlehem with a husband, two sons, and a heart filled with hope. Within ten years all her hopes were dashed and her family gone. She had only her two Moabite daughters-in-law left. Naomi heard that God had blessed Judah (the region Bethlehem was in) with good crops again, and she realized it was time to leave Moab and return to her homeland. One daughter-in-law, Ruth, decided to go with her.

When Naomi reached Bethlehem in Judah, the people recognized her even though she had aged. "Is it really Naomi?" her longtime friends asked each other. It had been ten years since they'd seen her, and they couldn't believe she'd returned.

"Don't call me Naomi," she said. "Call me Mara." The name Naomi means "pleasant," but Mara means "bitter," and Naomi felt bitter because of all that had happened. She told her friends and family in Bethlehem that she'd gone away full but had come home empty. Naomi had lost not one, but three close family members through death.

Coping with the death of someone close is hard. A flood of emotions hits you—denial, grief, guilt, bitterness, and maybe even relief, if the death follows a long illness. It can take years to work through those feelings.

In time, Naomi and Ruth were able to go on and have satisfying lives because they realized that God had more planned for them. Life was different, and there were still times of sadness, but they made new lives for themselves as they followed God's leading for their futures.

When you experience loss, take time to grieve. It's okay to feel sad. But don't let the sadness overwhelm you, because there is hope in Jesus. God journeys with you in sorrow, and in him, you can once again find joy.

Pray: Ask God to strengthen your faith for times of sorrow.

> I will never forget this awful time, as I grieve over my loss. Yet I still dare to hope when I remember this: The faithful love of the LORD never ends! His mercies never cease.
> LAMENTATIONS 3:20-22

A Life-Changing Journey

Read about Ruth's decision to go with Naomi in Ruth 1:6-18.

When the book of Ruth begins, Ruth is a young widow with an uncertain future. Being a widow in Bible times was hard. Widows were often ignored or taken advantage of. They lived in poverty unless there was someone to care for them. Under God's law, it was the responsibility of the dead husband's closest male relative to care for the widow, but in this case, Naomi, Orpah, and Ruth were alone in Moab. Naomi had no other sons to marry her daughters-in-law, and there were no male relatives to provide for the women.

Even in these desperate circumstances, we don't see any self-pity or bitterness in Ruth. Her concern is for her aging mother-in-law. Naomi wanted to return home to Bethlehem, where there was food and where some of her relatives perhaps were still alive. Ruth and Orpah began to go with her, but Orpah turned back at Naomi's urging. Not Ruth. She was determined to stay with Naomi. Ruth said, "Don't ask me to leave you and turn back. Wherever you go, I will go; wherever you live, I will live. Your people will be my people, and your God will be my God."

Ruth didn't know what to expect when she left her own home behind and made the long trek with Naomi to her land. There were new sights and places to see, the customs were different, and the Israelites worshiped the true God, not idols. Ruth bravely embraced this new land with its customs and people as her own.

In a way, that's what you do when you start your faith journey. You turn from your own way, believe in Jesus, and become part of his family. Your old, sinful ways are behind you, and you begin a new life following Jesus.

Pray: If you've already placed your faith in Jesus, thank him for giving you new life in him. If you haven't started your faith journey, consider telling God that you want to start today!

Anyone who belongs to Christ has become a new person.
The old life is gone; a new life has begun!
2 CORINTHIANS 5:17

Puzzle Page

*G*od has good plans for our lives! Decode the Telephone Puzzle below to read what the psalmist wrote about God's plan for his life.

Directions: This puzzle has two numbers under each blank. The first number matches one of the phone buttons. The second number tells you which letter on the button to write down. For instance, "9.3" means letter 3 on button 9. Check your answer below.

____ ____ ____ LORD ____ ____ ____ ____
8.1 4.2 3.2   9.1 4.3 5.3 5.3

____ ____ ____ ____ ____ ____ ____ his
9.1 6.3 7.3 5.2   6.3 8.2 8.1

____ ____ ____ ____ ____ ____ ____ ____ my
7.1 5.3 2.1 6.2 7.4   3.3 6.3 7.3

____ ____ ____ ____ — for ____ ____ ____ ____
5.3 4.3 3.3 3.2   9.3 6.3 8.2 7.3

____ ____ ____ ____ ____ ____ ____ ____   ____ ____ ____ ____ ,
3.3 2.1 4.3 8.1 4.2 3.3 8.2 5.3   5.3 6.3 8.3 3.2

____ LORD, ____ ____ ____ ____ ____ ____ ____ forever. Don't
6.3   3.2 6.2 3.1 8.2 7.3 3.2 7.4

____ ____ ____ ____ ____ ____ ____   ____ ____ , ____ ____ ____
2.1 2.2 2.1 6.2 3.1 6.3 6.2   6.1 3.2   3.3 6.3 7.3

____ ____ ____ ____ ____ ____ ____   ____ ____ .
9.3 6.3 8.2 6.1 2.1 3.1 3.2   6.1 3.2

1	2 ABC	3 DEF
4 GHI	5 JKL	6 MNO
7 PQRS	8 TUV	9 WXYZ
*	0 OPER	#

Hard Work Is Noticed

Read about Ruth working in Boaz's field in Ruth 2:1-23.

*R*uth and Naomi were two women alone without a way to care for themselves. Naomi was too old to work, so Ruth needed to find a way to provide for them. God's law said grain dropped by the harvesters as they gathered crops should be left for poor people to pick up. This was the perfect solution for Ruth.

One day Ruth went to collect grain in fields owned by a man named Boaz. She worked hard under the hot sun, gathering a small pile of grain, which grew larger as the day went on. She was determined to provide for both herself and Naomi and worked diligently to have a large supply of food. Ruth's hard work was quickly noticed by Boaz.

Boaz approached Ruth and spoke to her: "My daughter, listen to me. Don't go and glean in another field and don't go away from here. Stay here with my servant girls. Watch the field where the men are harvesting, and follow along after the girls. I have told the men not to touch you. And whenever you are thirsty, go and get a drink from the water jars the men have filled" (Ruth 2:8-9, NIV).

The conversation continued with Ruth asking Boaz why he was showing her this kindness, and he replied that he had heard of all she'd done for her mother-in-law and how she'd left her own land and journeyed with Naomi to a new country.

Ruth made an impression on Boaz through her hard work, loyalty to her mother-in-law, and her gracious manners, and later in the story, she becomes his wife. God used Boaz to rescue Ruth and Naomi, and Ruth and Boaz had a marriage blessed by God. Not only was their relationship blessed, but God also gave them a son named Obed, who was the grandfather of King David and an ancestor of Jesus.

Pray: Ask God to help you work hard for his glory, even if no one else seems to notice.

Work willingly at whatever you do, as though you were working for the Lord rather than for people. Remember that the Lord will give you an inheritance as your reward.
COLOSSIANS 3:23-24

God May Call You to Do Hard Things

Read God's blessing for those who trust him in hard times in Jeremiah 17:7-8.

God wants you to be willing to follow his plan for your life, but he doesn't promise it will be easy. In fact, I can't think of any Bible woman who had an easy, comfortable life and still made a difference to those around her. The Bible women who stand out are those who struggled with fear, discouragement, change, or hardship.

Hagar faced starvation in the desert. The midwives Shiphrah and Puah could have been killed for disobeying Pharaoh's orders to kill the Hebrew baby boys. Rahab risked her own life to help the spies. Deborah went into battle with the army. These women stand out because of the way they handled difficult situations with courage.

Rebekah traveled hundreds of miles to a new home to marry a man she'd never met. Jochebed gave up her son. Naomi left home because of a famine and returned, having buried her husband and two sons. Ruth left her homeland to live in Naomi's. These women stand out because of the noble way in which they faced the changes in their lives.

Each of these women had problems, but God worked through those difficulties to make them stronger. God may ask you to do something that is hard. Or you may face difficulties God allows. These don't catch God by surprise. He already knew you'd face them, and he knows how to help you through them. The important thing is to have faith in God during both the good times and the difficult ones.

Pray: Ask God to prepare you to do hard things for him.

> Don't be afraid, for I am with you. Don't be discouraged, for I am your God. I will strengthen you and help you. I will hold you up with my victorious right hand.
> ISAIAH 41:10

Quiz Time

*W*hat kind of worker are you? Rate yourself by reading each sentence and circling *A* for always, *S* for sometimes, or *N* for never.

1. I do my work without complaining.
   A S N

2. I am the first to volunteer when a job needs to be done.
   A S N

3. When I do a job, I give it my best.
   A S N

4. My parents and teachers would describe me as a hard worker.
   A S N

5. I am proud of the jobs I complete.
   A S N

How did you do? Give yourself 2 points for every *A*, 1 point for every *S*, and 0 points for every *N*.

Total _____

8–10 points: You are industrious like Ruth. You are hardworking and not afraid to tackle the tough jobs. You complete your tasks well and can be proud of your work. Be sure not to try to do it all yourself, though. Everyone needs help or a break at times.

5–7 points: You help out, but sometimes you slack off or leave the worst jobs for someone else. When you do your best, you can be proud of the work you do.

0–4 points: Too often you leave the work for someone else. You'd rather have fun than labor. Ask God to give you the desire to work hard and do your part. Give each job your best effort so you can be proud of the work, and others will notice too.

If you didn't score well, do your best with work this week and try the quiz again.

Power in Prayer

Read about Hannah's prayer for a son in 1 Samuel 1:1-18.

Hannah desperately wanted a son. Every year her family made a trip to the Tabernacle to worship and offer sacrifices. Hannah was deeply troubled by her inability to have any children, so she went into the Tabernacle alone to pour out her despair to God.

As she prayed, she promised God that if he blessed her with a son, she would give her son back to the Lord for his work. She loved God so much that she was willing to give him what she wanted most.

Eli the priest saw Hannah praying. She was praying with such passion that her lips were moving, but no sound was coming out, so Eli assumed she had come to the Tabernacle drunk!

Can you imagine how Hannah felt to be praying with such passion and to have the priest assume she was drunk? Hannah graciously explained to Eli that she was praying out of extreme sadness. Once Eli realized how wrongly he had judged Hannah, he quickly blessed her and asked God to grant her petition.

God already knew Hannah wanted a baby, so why did she have to keep praying? We don't always understand God's timing, but the Bible is clear that God loves when his children pour their hearts out to him as Hannah did.

When you get close to God through prayer, you will desire the things he wants for you, and you will sense him guiding you on the path he's chosen for you. That doesn't mean you won't have any more problems, but it does mean that God will lead you through them or will give you the power to overcome them.

Pray: Talk to God about the desires of your heart.

> Rejoice in our confident hope. Be patient in trouble,
> and keep on praying.
> **ROMANS 12:12**

Giving Back to God

Read about Hannah's courageous choice to give her son back to God in 1 Samuel 1:24–2:11.

*W*hen Samuel was just a young boy, Hannah kept her promise to God and took him to live at the Tabernacle with Eli the priest.

It was probably difficult for Hannah to leave Samuel with the priest. Eli was elderly, and his sons were wicked. First Samuel 2 describes them as "scoundrels who had no respect for the LORD or for their duties as priests" (verses 12-13). Yet Hannah left her child because she knew Samuel was really in God's care. Hannah gave her firstborn son to God not out of duty but out of joy, because of her love for God and her gratitude for his answer to her prayer.

What do you have that you could give to God? You don't have children to dedicate to God, but how about your time? Could you set aside some time to help an elderly neighbor mow her lawn as an act of service to God? Or could you play with your younger sibling for an hour to give your parents a break out of love for God? Maybe you could use your time on Saturday morning to help clean the church or pull weeds.

How about your talents? Are there things you are good at that you could give back to God? If you're musical, perhaps you could help with children's choir or sing in the youth choir. If you're good with children, maybe you could be a teacher's assistant for vacation Bible school.

Perhaps you babysit or have a part-time summer job. You can give some of your money to God's work.

Hannah bravely gave her son to the Lord. What can you give to God?

Pray: Ask God to show you how you can serve him and to help you to be faithful in what he has called you to do.

> "I asked the LORD to give me this boy, and he has granted my request. Now I am giving him to the LORD, and he will belong to the LORD his whole life." And they worshiped the LORD there.
> **1 SAMUEL 1:27-28**

Puzzle Page

*H*annah poured out her heart to God in prayer. Solve the Thermometer Puzzle to find out what the Bible says we should do with our sadness and worries.

Directions: Look at the thermometer. Each temperature has a corresponding letter. Look at the temperatures under the lines below. Above each line, write the letter that goes with the temperature. Check your answers below.

__ __ __ __   __ __ __   __ __ __ __
30° 40° 80° 25° 5° 45° 45° 90° 55° 75° 60°

__ __ __ __ __ __ __   __ __ __
85° 55° 60° 60° 40° 25° 65° 5° 50° 20°

__ __ __ __ __   __ __   __ __ __ , for he
15° 5° 60° 25° 65° 70° 55° 30° 55° 20°

__ __ __ __ __   __ __ __ __ __
15° 5° 60° 25° 65° 5° 10° 55° 75° 70°

__ __ __ .
90° 55° 75°

Temp	Letter
90	Y
85	W
80	V
75	U
70	T
65	S
60	R
55	O
50	N
45	L
40	I
35	H
30	G
25	E
20	D
15	C
10	B
5	A

Wisdom from God

Read about Abigail's wise thinking in 1 Samuel 25:1-38.

*W*as Abigail born with the wisdom to know how to defuse the situation between Nabal and David? Did she instinctively know to hurry and prepare food? Did the words she spoke to David to prevent him from committing murder just flow from her lips? No, they came from a lifetime of seeking God, following him, and trusting him to work out the circumstances of her life.

Many people try to be wise on their own, but according to James 3:13-16, they are jealous and are trying to get ahead in the world. They boast, lie, and seek all the world has to offer. That kind of wisdom might get them ahead in the short term, but it doesn't score any points with God.

How do you develop the true kind of wisdom? By getting to know God better. You can do this by spending time reading the Bible and praying every day and participating in your church.

When you are faced with a decision, pray about what God wants you to do. Look in the Bible to see if you can find any verses that talk about the situation. Talk to adults who are mature Christians.

Ask yourself what God would want you to do in each situation, and do it even if it's not the popular thing. When you listen for God's leading, you will sense his guidance in your heart, through your conscience. When you regularly ask God to direct you, listen for his leading, and then follow it, you will find wise actions coming naturally to you. That is how Abigail was able to quickly take action and save the day for her household, and it will help you, too.

Pray: Ask God to help you make wise decisions.

> The LORD grants wisdom! From his mouth come knowledge and understanding.
> PROVERBS 2:6

Giving without Fear

Read about the bold generosity of the widow of Zarephath in 1 Kings 17:8-16.

*T*he widow of Zarephath and her son lived in their own house but had few possessions. She probably had a small barley field and a few olive trees. When the harvest was good, she had enough food to care for herself and her child, but there was a drought, and nothing was growing. She had no way to care for herself and her son. The two of them were down to their last meal before they would die.

During this time, the prophet Elijah was on the run from people who wanted him dead. Elijah went to the widow's town and saw her gathering sticks. He asked her for a drink of water and a bite of bread.

Can you imagine what went through this woman's mind? She was scrimping together the end of her flour for one last meal, and a stranger asked her for bread. What would you have said? "Are you kidding? I don't even have enough for myself." Or maybe, "Who are you, and why are you asking me for food? Why don't you bring me some food?"

Elijah told her not to be afraid. Then he told her to give him food first. First? Why was this man taking advantage of a starving woman?

Elijah assured her she'd have flour and oil until her own crops grew again. The woman had a decision to make—give the rest of her food to Elijah on faith she'd receive more, or use it for herself and her son as she had planned. The widow chose to give all she had left to Elijah in faith.

God chose to use a poor woman to help the prophet Elijah. She had faith in what he said, and her flour and olive oil were never gone until the drought was over—just as God had promised.

Be like the widow and be ready to give generously and without fear when God prompts you. God wants to bless you and use your giving as an encouragement to others.

Pray: Ask God to make you a brave, cheerful, and generous giver.

> Give, and you will receive. Your gift will return to you in full—pressed down, shaken together to make room for more, running over, and poured into your lap. The amount you give will determine the amount you get back.
>
> LUKE 6:38

Puzzle Page

Solve the Thermometer Puzzle below to read a verse about generosity.

Directions: Look at the thermometer. Each temperature has a corresponding letter. Look at the temperatures under the lines below. Above each line, write the letter that goes with the temperature. Check your answers below.

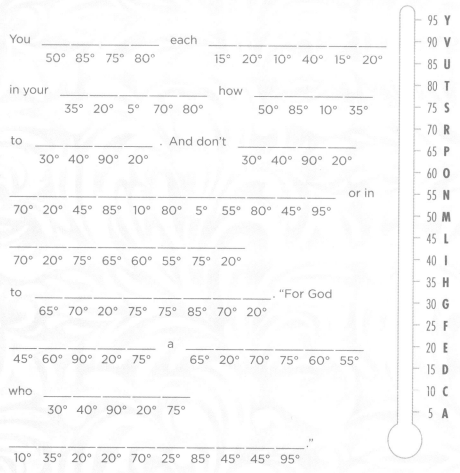

You _____ each _____
    50° 85° 75° 80°   15° 20° 10° 40° 15° 20°

in your _____ how _____
    35° 20° 5° 70° 80°   50° 85° 10° 35°

to _____ . And don't _____
   30° 40° 90° 20°   30° 40° 90° 20°

_____ or in
70° 20° 45° 85° 10° 80° 5° 55° 80° 45° 95°

_____
70° 20° 75° 65° 60° 55° 75° 20°

to _____ . "For God
  65° 70° 20° 75° 75° 85° 70° 20°

_____ a _____
45° 60° 90° 20° 75°   65° 20° 70° 75° 60° 55°

who _____
   30° 40° 90° 20° 75°

_____ ."
10° 35° 20° 20° 70° 25° 85° 45° 45° 95°

Temp	Letter
95	Y
90	V
85	U
80	T
75	S
70	R
65	P
60	O
55	N
50	M
45	L
40	I
35	H
30	G
25	F
20	E
15	D
10	C
5	A

How might this verse have applied to the widow of Zarephath? How does it apply to you?

Stepping Out in Faith

Read about the widow's miraculous supply of oil in 2 Kings 4:1-7.

O ne day a widow with two boys went to find Elisha, a prophet of God, to get his help. The woman owed money, and the creditor was going to take her sons as slaves in payment.

Elisha asked the woman what she had in her home, and she told him she had only a little oil. Elisha instructed her to ask the neighbors for as many empty jars as were available. He told her to then go into her house, shut the door, and pour her oil into the pots. The widow did as Elisha said. She poured from her oil jar, filling each pot until there were no more. Then the oil stopped. Elisha told the woman to sell the oil, pay her debt, and use the rest to live on.

The widow sought out Elisha because he was a man of God, and she believed he could help solve her problem, but she didn't know how he would do it. His instructions to her may have seemed strange, but she did exactly as he said. The woman went house to hou borrowing empty jars. I wonder what she told the neighbors when she borrowed them. "The man of God said I should borrow these"? "I'm expecting a miraculous flow of oil"? We don't know what she said, but we know she had faith that what Elisha said really would happen.

The widow's faith saved her from her creditor. It kept her from losing her sons, who would have become servants to the creditor. Her faith not only paid her debts, but it also gave her money to support herself and her sons until they were grown and could care for her.

Just like the widow of Zarephath, this widow believed in God's provision, and God did not disappoint her. When is the last time you stepped out in faith, trusting God for something specific? If you were in the widow's situation, would your faith take you door-to-door collecting as many jars as you could? Or would you just collect one or two jars to test whether the oil really would keep flowing?

Pray: Ask the Holy Spirit to give you the boldness to step out in faith.

> When all the jars were full, she said to her son, "Bring me another one." But he replied, "There is not a jar left." Then the oil stopped flowing.
> 2 KINGS 4:6, NIV

Telling Others about God

Read about the young servant girl's compassion for her master in 2 Kings 5:1-19.

*T*he young servant was an Israelite being raised by godly parents. During a raid on the Israelites, the girl was taken, and she ended up in Naaman's house as a personal servant to his wife. Over time, the girl came to care about Naaman and his wife.

Though Naaman was an important man, he had leprosy, a skin disease. One day the young servant remarked to her mistress that she wished Naaman would go see the prophet Elisha in Samaria. She knew that God could work miracles and could heal Naaman of his disease. Naaman told his king what the girl had said, and the king told him to go. This was the first spark of hope for a cure for Naaman.

The young servant was a captive, taken from her parents and brought to a foreign land. The servant girl could have been bitter. She could have wondered why God didn't either rescue her or punish those who captured her. She even could have rejoiced that Naaman had leprosy—but she didn't. She had God's love in her heart and a strong faith instilled by her parents. She knew no matter where she was, God was looking out for her. She trusted he would fulfill his plan for her, whether it was to go home or to stay in Naaman's house.

Elisha gave Naaman instructions to wash in the Jordan River, and his leprosy was healed. Naaman declared, "Now I know that there is no God in all the world except in Israel" (2 Kings 5:15). Because the young Hebrew servant was brave enough to speak to Naaman's wife, Naaman was healed and he worshiped God.

If you, like the young servant girl, are often surrounded by peers who don't believe in God, you have a chance to talk to them about your faith. When did you last talk to a classmate or friend about God?

Pray: Ask God for an opportunity to tell someone about him this week.

> No one lights a lamp and then puts it under a basket. Instead, a lamp is placed on a stand, where it gives light to everyone in the house. In the same way, let your good deeds shine out for all to see, so that everyone will praise your heavenly Father.
> MATTHEW 5:15-16

Quiz Time

The young servant girl used a challenging situation to share the gospel with her master instead of being bitter toward him. You can determine that you will make the best of the situations that come your way and allow God to use you in them. Take the quiz below to see how well you do that. Rate yourself by reading each sentence and circling *A* for always, *S* for sometimes, or *N* for never.

1. I understand when I have to change my personal plans due to family plans.
   A S N

2. I handle it with dignity when I am left out of a friend's plans.
   A S N

3. I realize things don't have to revolve around me.
   A S N

4. I let my brother or sister have his or her way some of the time without complaining.
   A S N

5. I can deal with it when plans are canceled or changed due to rain, sickness, or lack of money.
   A S N

How did you do? Give yourself 2 points for every *A*, 1 point for every *S*, and 0 points for every *N*.

8–10 points: Good for you. You understand that there are things you can't control, and you accept the disappointments and changes graciously.

5–7 points: You try to accept the disruptions and changes to your plans, but you sometimes react negatively to those things. Learn to accept the things that can't be changed. Trust God to work through those things.

0–4 points: Allow God to work in your heart to help you accept circumstances you can't change. Ask God to give you a gracious spirit when things don't go your way.

Saying No

Read about Queen Vashti's refusal to appear at her husband's party in Esther 1:1-12.

The first chapter of Esther reads like a drama. The stage is set. The actors are in place—King Xerxes and the men partying for a week, and the women with Queen Vashti at a smaller banquet. The king, proud of all he owns and looking for attention from all his friends, decides it's now time to show off his most beautiful "possession" of all—his wife.

In the next scene, the women watch as several men tell the queen what the king expects. The women wait to hear what Vashti will do. They recognize that it is a downright disgusting request, but the request also comes from the king. Refusing will surely have serious consequences.

Vashti, with more concern for her dignity and integrity than her royal standing, refuses to go to the king.

Similar dramas play out around you daily. The key players are you and your peers. Every day you face decisions. Will you make fun of someone else to secure your position with the in-crowd, or risk being ignored? Will you go to a classmate's party to raise your social status even though you know the movies they plan to watch aren't appropriate? Will you take a peek at the answer key someone handed around before the science test because it might be your only chance to pass? Will you hang out with a group in the neighborhood just to have friends even though the things they talk about embarrass you?

Queen Vashti decided her dignity and integrity were more important than the riches she had as queen. Are you willing to make the right choices and be a role model even though it might mean losing social status or being alone more than you'd like? Or could you find someone to make the right choices with you—and make a new friend in the process?

Pray: Ask God to give you the courage to say no to temptation.

> When they conveyed the king's order to Queen Vashti, she refused to come. This made the king furious, and he burned with anger.
> **ESTHER 1:12**

Working Out for Good

Read about the king's response to Queen Vashti in Esther 1:13-22.

*W*hen Vashti failed to appear before the king, it made the king look foolish in front of the other men. What kind of king couldn't even get his wife to obey him? The king's advisers suggested he banish Vashti. They were fearful that when all the other women in the kingdom heard she'd refused the king, they would refuse to do what their husbands asked them to do also. So Vashti was no longer queen.

With Vashti gone, the king searched for a new queen, and Esther was selected. The choice of queen shows God's hand in the lives of his people, because Esther, a Jew, was on the throne at just the right time to save her people from harm. God used for good what seemed like a tragedy—Vashti being banished.

God is able to take a bad situation and turn it around in order to accomplish good. Sometimes it's hard to see how any good could come out of a situation, and we may not always know what God is up to. Vashti probably didn't see how any good would come from her being sent away, but God could see the whole picture.

God is in control even when we don't see it. He has better things planned for us than we can ever imagine. Our job is to have faith and obey God, trusting him to work things out. He promises to bless our obedience and accomplish his purposes.

Pray: Thank God that his plans can always be trusted.

> "For I know the plans I have for you," says the LORD. "They are plans for good and not for disaster, to give you a future and a hope."
> JEREMIAH 29:11

Puzzle Page

*D*ecode the verses in the puzzle below to read what God says about his ways in the book of Isaiah.

Directions: The words in the word bank fit into the boxes below. The best way to solve these puzzles is to start with the longest words first. Then, if you have many short words with the same number of letters left, you can fill them in based on which word makes sense in each box. Give it a try.

anything	ways (3)	beyond		imagine	higher (3)	far
could	heavens	thoughts (2)	just	earth		

My ___ ___ ___ ___ are ___ ___ ___ ___ ___ ___ ___ ___ ___

___ ___ ___ ___ ___ ___ ___ you ___ ___ ___ ___ ___

___ ___ ___ ___ ___ ___ ___ . For ___ ___ ___ ___ as the

___ ___ ___ ___ ___ ___ ___ are ___ ___ ___ ___ ___ ___

than the ___ ___ ___ ___ ___ , so my ___ ___ ___ ___ are

___ ___ ___ ___ ___ than your ___ ___ ___ ___ and

my ___ ___ ___ ___ ___ ___ ___ ___ ___ ___ ___ ___ ___ ___

than your ___ ___ ___ ___ ___ ___ ___ ___ .

For Such a Time as This

Read about Mordecai's conversation with Esther in Esther 4:1-17.

God had a plan for Esther before she was even born. He knew one day she would be married to the king and be in a position to save her people.

Esther's cousin Mordecai found out about a plan by King Xerxes's adviser Haman to kill all the Jewish people. Mordecai told Esther she had to speak to the king and get him to help the Jews. He told Esther that God might have put her in the palace for just that reason.

God arranged for Esther to be right where she needed to be when she needed to be there. God could have just zapped Haman for his evil plan, but that's not the way he works. If God wiped out everyone who had a wicked thought, the world would be empty. God allows bad things to happen because we live on a sinful earth. Haman followed his own sinful nature. But God also had a plan to save his people, and that plan centered on Esther. She was in the palace "for just such a time as this."

Each of us is created with a purpose. Our purposes may not seem as grand as Esther's, but they are important just the same. Knowing that God has a purpose for you will change the way you live. Instead of moping around doing nothing, you will be engaged in seeking what he wants you to do. There's no secret formula to finding out his plan for you. You just need to be willing to be used by God, stay attentive to his voice in your heart and in the Bible, and then do things that are pleasing to him.

Pray: Tell God you are willing to be used by him to accomplish his purposes.

> If you keep quiet at a time like this, deliverance and relief for the Jews will arise from some other place, but you and your relatives will die. Who knows if perhaps you were made queen for just such a time as this?
> **ESTHER 4:14**

True Courage

Read about Esther bravely approaching the king in Esther 5:1-8.

*H*aman devised a plan to kill all the Jews, including Mordecai and possibly Esther (though she had kept her Jewish heritage a secret). Mordecai told Esther that she needed to talk to the king and plead for her people. But you couldn't just walk up to the king and ask him for a favor. You had to wait for him to send for you. If Esther approached the king without being summoned, she could be killed.

Esther agreed to approach the king, but she told Mordecai to gather the Jews and have them fast and pray for her for three days. And in a moment of true courage she declared, "If I must die, I must die."

Esther had courage because she knew she was doing the right thing. Approaching the king was necessary to save herself and her people. Perhaps there has been a time when you had to stand up to peers who wanted you to do something wrong. Or maybe you befriended another student, knowing that others might ignore you or make fun of you for it. You can do those things bravely, knowing they are choices that honor God.

Esther also had courage because she was prepared when she faced the king. Esther didn't impulsively run to the king and blurt out her problem. She stopped to think things through and make a plan. Maybe you have a speech contest or play audition coming up, or you plan to ask the principal for permission to start a Bible club. When you are prepared, you can approach the situation with courage.

Finally, Esther had courage because she knew the outcome was in God's hands. Knowing that God is in control gives you added courage to face the tough times in your life.

Follow Esther's example next time you have to do something that requires bravery.

Pray: Ask God to give you the courage to do what is right.

> Go and gather together all the Jews of Susa and fast for me. Do not eat or drink for three days, night or day. My maids and I will do the same. And then, though it is against the law, I will go in to see the king. If I must die, I must die.
> ESTHER 4:16

Puzzle Page

God has good plans for us, just as he had good plans for Esther. Solve the puzzle below to see what the Bible says about our part in God's plans.

Directions: The words in the word bank fit into the boxes below. The best way to solve these puzzles is to start with the longest words first. Then, if you have many short words with the same number of letters left, you can fill them in based on which word makes sense in each box. Give it a try.

planned	has	good	can	are	created
masterpiece	For	ago	God's	Jesus	things
for	us	anew	we	Christ	long

__ __ __ we __ __ __ __ __ __ __ __' __

__ __ __ __ __ __ __ __ __ __ __ __ . He __ __ __

__ __ __ __ __ __ us __ __ __ __ in

__ __ __ __ __ __ __ __ __ __ , so __ __

__ __ do the __ __ __ __ __ __ __ __

he __ __ __ __ __ __ __ __ __ __ __ __

__ __ __ __ __ __ __ .

What has God done for us?

Facing Fear

Read about how God used Esther to save the Jews in Esther 7:1–8:17.

*E*sther had every right to be afraid—of the extermination of her people and of her own death from appearing before the king without being summoned first. She wasn't a great leader or warrior; she was a young Jewish girl, alone except for an older cousin. She was the queen only because the king was taken with her beauty. It was normal for her to be afraid.

Fear is natural, but like Esther, you don't have to let it keep you from doing what you need to do. Sometimes fear is helpful. It's an emotion that's programmed into your nervous system and alerts you when there is danger. Your brain kicks into gear and causes your body to respond by making your heart beat faster and your breathing become more rapid. Blood pressure rises and skin sweats to keep the body cool. Your muscles prepare to run or fight. The fear prepares you to face the approaching danger.

Fear becomes a problem when it keeps you from doing what you need to do. Esther felt afraid when Mordecai told her she needed to approach the king, but it didn't keep her from acting.

Rather than avoiding what you are afraid of, face it head-on. Name your fear. Then prepare for situations when you might face your fear.

Afraid to share your faith? Practice different methods that are comfortable for you, like telling a peer what God has done for you.

Scared of the dark? Think of the reason you might be afraid. If you know you will be outside in the dark, bring a flashlight with extra batteries.

Afraid to speak in front of others? Practice giving your report to your family or a group of friends until you can do it with ease.

Fill your mind with Scripture, and ask God to fill your heart with courage.

Pray: Ask God to take away any fear that is keeping you from whole-heartedly following him.

> God has not given us a spirit of fear and timidity, but of power, love, and self-discipline.
> **2 TIMOTHY 1:7**

Remembering

Read about the Jews celebrating the Festival of Purim in Esther 9:16-32.

Esther was a hero to the Jews because she talked to King Xerxes about Haman's plot to destroy them. The king gave the Jews permission to defend themselves against their enemies, and when the time came, the king allowed them two days to fight their enemies. Instead of the Jews being annihilated, they defeated those who wanted to kill them.

Mordecai said that the Jews should hold a celebration each year on the two days when the Jews defeated their enemies. The celebration is called the Festival of Purim, named after the lots, or dice, that Haman cast to choose the day to kill the Jews. Celebrating the Festival of Purim helps the Jews remember Esther's story as they retell it each year.

Remembering special events is important because it draws our attention to God's work in our lives. Jews still celebrate Purim to remind them of God's faithfulness.

Think of a time when you or your family saw God at work. Have a celebration and remember what God did for you. It could be a party with your family or just a time when you thank God and share what he's done for you.

What has God done for you that you want to remember?

Pray: Praise God for the ways he has cared for you in the past.

> Your awe-inspiring deeds will be on every tongue; I will proclaim your greatness. Everyone will share the story of your wonderful goodness; they will sing with joy about your righteousness.
> **PSALM 145:6-7**

Puzzle Page

*U*se the Box Code below to help you decode the verse. See how God wants to bless your desire to be brave for him.

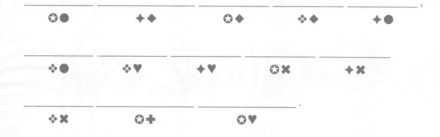

	♦	●	♥	✖	✚
✪	in	Take	desires	give	heart's
✦	delight	LORD	will	you	
❖	the	and	he	your	

____ ____ ____ ____ ____ ,
  ✪●   ✦♦   ✪♦   ❖♦   ✦●

____ ____ ____ ____ ____
  ❖●   ❖♥   ✦♥   ✪✖   ✦✖

____ ____ ____ .
  ❖✖   ✪✚   ✪♥

God Sees the Whole Plan

Read about God having a plan for you before you were even born in Psalm 139:1-16.

Ever do a jigsaw puzzle? At first you have one hundred or more colorful pieces scattered on the table. Then you start assembling the border. You get the framework in place for the puzzle. Then, one piece at a time, you start putting the picture together using the box cover as a guide. Have you ever tried to assemble a puzzle without the picture as a guide? It might not be too difficult with a one-hundred-piece puzzle, but just try it with a five-hundred-piece puzzle! Without knowing what the puzzle should look like, you'd just have hundreds of colorful pieces. Is that blue piece part of the sky? A lake? Flowers in a field?

Sometimes life feels like a jigsaw puzzle with no picture. You see bits and pieces of your life, but you don't know what the whole picture looks like. You have a problem with a teacher. You finally get a B on a math test. Your grandmother gets sick. You find out you're moving. You score the winning soccer goal. All these pieces are part of your life, but you only see them a piece at a time. God sees the whole thing. He knows what the picture of your life looks like and how all the pieces fit together.

Esther's story is a good example of this. Vashti refused to follow the king's order and was banished. The king held an elaborate beauty contest to choose a new queen. A young Jewish woman was chosen. Then her cousin Mordecai found out about a plot to kill all the Jews. He told Esther she had to tell the king. He said she might have been chosen just so she'd be in place to save her people. That's how God works. He sees the whole picture of our lives, and he arranges the pieces so they all fit together to form that picture.

You see your life one piece at a time. You live your life one day at a time. God will lead you day by day on the path he wants you to take if you ask him to.

Pray: Thank God that you can never mess up his plans for your life.

> You saw me before I was born. Every day of my life was recorded in your book. Every moment was laid out before a single day had passed.
> PSALM 139:16

Be Strong and Courageous

Read about God's help and protection in Psalm 27:1-14.

T he Bible is full of women who faced and overcame fear. Several of the women you've already read about in this book faced fearful situations:

Shiphrah and Puah disobeyed an order to kill all the Hebrew baby boys, which could have meant their own deaths if they were found out.

Jochebed placed baby Moses in a basket in the river because she feared for her young son's life.

Ruth traveled with her mother-in-law to a new country with unfamiliar customs.

Hannah waited for years for a son and then made the heart-breaking choice to give him back to God.

Abigail thought her husband was going to be murdered.

The widow of Zarephath feared that both she and her son would starve to death.

Vashti refused to present herself at the king's party and risked losing her role as queen.

Esther could have been killed for appearing before the king without his permission.

All of these women had their own fears and anxieties, but all of them trusted in God and knew that whatever happened was part of God's plan for them. They had faith in the face of danger, change, or the unknown. And in every case, God blessed them because of it.

Are you facing a situation that is causing you to be anxious or afraid? Think of the brave Bible women you've read about and trust God to work things out for you just as he did for each of them.

Pray: Thank God for his faithfulness to the courageous women of the Bible, and to you.

Be strong and courageous! Do not be afraid and do not panic before them. For the LORD your God will personally go ahead of you. He will neither fail you nor abandon you.
DEUTERONOMY 31:6

Quiz Time

*Y*ou've read about many Bible women who bravely followed God. Do you remember who is who? Take the quiz below to see how well you remember the Bible women so far.

Eve	Ruth	Shiphrah and Puah	
Esther	Deborah	Sarah	Rebekah
Jochebed	Miriam	Rahab	Hannah
Vashti	Hagar	Naomi	Abigail

Choose the correct answer from above.

1. Although not Abraham's wife, she gave birth to his first son.
   _____

2. She hung a red cord from her window in order to save herself and her family. _____

3. She collected grain to support herself and her mother-in-law.
   _____

4. She listened to the serpent rather than God and had to leave her garden home. _____

5. She had her first and only child at the age of ninety. _____

6. After her husband acted foolishly, she wisely saved her household. _____

7. She went before the king without being invited. _____

8. These brave women refused to kill the Hebrew baby boys.
   _____

9. She returned to Israel after the death of her husband and son.
   _____

10. She traveled five hundred miles to marry someone she had never met. _____

11. When she could no longer keep her infant son safe, she set him afloat in the river. _____

12. She helped her brother lead the Hebrews out of Egypt.
_____

13. She led Israel as a judge. _____

14. She gave her long-awaited son back to God. _____

15. When the king wanted to show her off at his party, she refused.
_____

Perfect Timing

Read about God's promise to give Elizabeth a son in Luke 1:5-25.

Being unable to have children in Bible times was shameful. People usually thought of it as a sign of God's displeasure. Zechariah and Elizabeth obeyed God in all they did, yet they hadn't had any children in all the years they'd been married. They were probably perplexed by why God hadn't sent them children.

Like the Old Testament women before her, Elizabeth pleaded with God for a child. But many years passed, and she did not get pregnant. Although disappointed not to have children, she and her husband stayed faithful to God and were busy serving him. Then, as with Sarah and Abraham, an angel delivered surprising news. Elizabeth would have a baby even though she was past the age when it seemed possible.

God sent a baby to Elizabeth at the exact time he'd planned. It wasn't an afterthought. He didn't suddenly change his mind and decide to send a child after all. It was part of his plan from the beginning. God's thoughts and ways are far beyond ours, so we can't always understand why he does the things he does. God just wants us to wait on him and trust him to work in our lives. This doesn't mean we should simply sit and wait. We can serve him while he reveals his plan for us one day at a time.

Pray: Ask God to help you trust that his timing is perfect.

> "My thoughts are nothing like your thoughts," says the LORD.
> "And my ways are far beyond anything you could imagine.
> For just as the heavens are higher than the earth, so my ways
> are higher than your ways and my thoughts higher than your
> thoughts."
> ISAIAH 55:8-9

Equipped for a Job

Read about the birth of Elizabeth's son, John, in Luke 1:57-80.

*E*lizabeth knew her baby would be special because God had performed a miracle in order for her to become pregnant. Her son had a special mission, and she was given specific instructions about how to raise him. Zechariah was told these things by the angel:

You are to name him John. (Normally children were named for a relative, but there was no one named John in Zechariah's family.)

You will have great joy and gladness.

Many will rejoice at his birth.

He will be great in the eyes of the Lord.

He must never touch wine or other alcoholic drinks.

He will be filled with the Holy Spirit, even before his birth.

He will turn many Israelites to the Lord their God.

He will be a man with the spirit and power of Elijah.

He will prepare the people for the coming of the Lord.

He will turn the hearts of the fathers to their children.

He will cause those who are rebellious to accept the wisdom of the godly.

When God chooses someone to do a job for him, he makes sure that person is equipped for the task. John the Baptist had the important mission of preaching about the Savior in order to prepare people to trust in Jesus. Zechariah and Elizabeth had the righteousness and maturity to raise their special son.

When God asks you to do something for him, you can be confident, knowing he has already enabled you for the job.

Pray: Thank God for equipping you to do what he has asked of you.

By his divine power, God has given us everything we need for living a godly life. We have received all of this by coming to know him, the one who called us to himself by means of his marvelous glory and excellence.

2 PETER 1:3

Puzzle Page

*E*lizabeth was heartbroken that she couldn't have a child, but God turned her sadness into joy. Solve the Speedometer Puzzle below to see what the Bible says about sad times.

Directions: Each blank line has a number under it. Those numbers correspond to a letter on the speedometer. Decode the words and check your answer below.

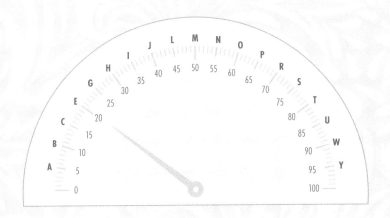

___ ___ ___ ___ ___ ___ ___   ___ ___ ___   ___ ___ ___ ___
90   20   20   65   35   55   25   50   5   95   45   5   75   80

___ ___ ___ ___ ___ ___ ___   the   ___ ___ ___ ___ ___ ,
80   30   70   60   85   25   30   55   35   25   30   80

___ ___ ___   ___ ___ ___ . ___ ___ ___ ___ ___
10   85   80   40   60   95   15   60   50   20   75

with the   ___ ___ ___ ___ ___ ___ ___ .
           50   60   70   55   35   55   25

The Lord's Servant

Read about the angel Gabriel visiting Mary in Luke 1:26-38.

ary. was an ordinary girl whose life was probably much the same as any other girl's in the small village of Nazareth. She never dreamed that in one day her whole life would change. Mary may have been grinding grain or preparing a meal, or she may have been getting ready for bed or daydreaming about her upcoming marriage to Joseph when an angel appeared to her and told her she would be the mother of the Savior.

This was shocking news to Mary. She loved God and believed the prophecies that the Messiah would one day be born, but she never dreamed she would be the one to give birth to him. Yet she accepted the angel's news and only asked how she, a virgin and unmarried girl, could give birth to the Son of God. It would have been understandable if she had asked more questions like "What will I tell people when they realize I'm pregnant but not married?" and "How do I explain this to Joseph?" But Mary simply acknowledged she was God's servant and would do as he asked.

Mary accepted God's plan for her even though it meant having to explain her pregnancy to friends and family, risking people thinking she had sinned, having her friends fail to believe her news, making a long journey to talk things over with her relative Elizabeth, making another long journey for a census right at the time the baby would be born, and watching her son grow up to be rejected and crucified. Of course, Mary didn't know all of this ahead of time, but certainly she sensed her life would be anything but easy and typical from this point on.

Mary accepted God's plan for her because she had a strong faith in him and trusted him totally. Are you able to accept and willingly do the things God asks of you, knowing his plan for you is best?

Pray: Ask God to give you a willing heart to obey him.

> Mary responded, "I am the Lord's servant. May everything you have said about me come true." And then the angel left her.
> **LUKE 1:38**

Accepting God's Plan

Read Mary's response of praise in Luke 1:46-55.

Before Gabriel's visit, Mary didn't know what God's plan for her was, other than to love and serve him, learn the Scriptures, and obey them. That is what Mary was doing when God told her she would give birth to Jesus.

When Mary learned that God's will for her was to be the mother of Jesus, it was a major, life-changing event. But most of the time, knowing and doing God's will is a day-by-day experience. God may have chosen Mary for the big task because she was faithful to obey God in little things. This showed God she had a willing heart.

The same is true today. God has a plan for you, but he may not reveal it to you all at once. Are you willing to accept God's will for your life? God may want you to be a missionary or a teacher. He may plan for you to be a professional singer or athlete. God may choose you to create computer programs or sell clothing. He probably won't send an angel to give you the plan in person, but he will lead you toward this plan day by day, step by step. The things you are learning in school and at home this week may be the very things you'll need to know to fulfill God's plan for you.

Each morning, ask God to show you his plan for you for that day, and then try to do the things you know he wants you to do. It may be as easy as asking a new student to be your partner in PE class or obeying your mom when she asks you to do the dishes. When you are faithful to do these little things, God will see your willingness and courage and will give you bigger things to do for him.

Pray: Ask God to lead you through your day today.

> Mary responded, "Oh, how my soul praises the Lord. How my spirit rejoices in God my Savior! For he took notice of his lowly servant girl, and from now on all generations will call me blessed. For the Mighty One is holy, and he has done great things for me."
> LUKE 1:46-49

Quiz Time

*M*ary obeyed God. How well do you obey? Read each question below, and circle *A* for always, *S* for sometimes, or *N* for never.

1. I obey the first time I'm told to do something.
   A   S   N

2. I follow my parents' rules even if they won't know the difference.
   A   S   N

3. I accept my parents' decisions even if I don't agree.
   A   S   N

4. If I disagree with a rule, I talk it out respectfully with my parents.
   A   S   N

How did you do? Give yourself 2 points for every *A*, 1 point for every *S*, and 0 points for every *N*.

6-8 points: You do a good job of obeying your parents. Praise God for the way he's at work in your heart!

3-5 points: You try to obey, but there is room for improvement. Ask for God's help to keep growing in obedience.

0-2 points: Obedience is a struggle for you. In John 14:15, Jesus says, "If you love me, obey my commandments." The way you obey your parents reflects your love for God. But God loves to help us in our areas of weakness, so don't despair!

The Savior Is Born

Read about the birth of Jesus in Luke 2:1-20.

The time had come. The long-awaited Messiah was born in a stable in Bethlehem, because all the inns were full. Jesus' arrival wasn't a grand birth into a noble or wealthy family. Just young Mary and Joseph the carpenter were there, alone in a stable. The only eyewitnesses to the birth were the barn animals that may have been present. But this is how God planned it from the beginning. Second Corinthians 8:9 says, "Though he was rich, yet for your sakes he became poor, so that by his poverty he could make you rich." Jesus chose to give up his heavenly riches to come to earth for you. He didn't come to save just the rich or famous but the everyday people who work hard to make ends meet.

God often works through the lowly things of life to accomplish his will. First Corinthians 1:27 says, "God chose the foolish things of the world to shame the wise" (NIV). God chooses the weak and lowly because they know they need him. The rich and powerful may take credit for their own successes rather than acknowledging God's work in their lives.

We are encouraged to have the same attitude Jesus had on earth—that of a servant. Philippians 2:5-8 says, "You must have the same attitude that Christ Jesus had. Though he was God, he did not think of equality with God as something to cling to. Instead, he gave up his divine privileges. . . . He humbled himself in obedience to God and died a criminal's death on a cross."

Jesus, God's own Son, came to earth through a lowly birth and lived a servant's life in order to be the sacrifice for our sins. He didn't set himself up as an earthly king with great riches. He became part of Mary and Joseph's family because they were willing to lay aside their own plans and expectations to live out God's will.

Pray: Thank God for coming to earth to save you from your sins and give you new life in him.

> She gave birth to her firstborn, a son. She wrapped him in cloths and placed him in a manger, because there was no room for them in the inn.
> LUKE 2:7, NIV

Simeon's Prophecy

Read about the grief Mary was prophesied to endure in Luke 2:25-35.

Simeon was a righteous elderly man who was eagerly awaiting the coming of the Messiah. God had revealed to him that he wouldn't die until he'd seen the Savior. One day God urged him to go to the Temple. It was the same day that Joseph and Mary took Jesus to the Temple to present him as the law required. Simeon recognized Jesus as the Messiah and took him in his arms. He praised God, and then he said something that must have caused Mary concern: "A sword will pierce your very soul."

Mary knew that nothing could happen to Jesus that his heavenly Father didn't allow, but God hadn't told her what Jesus' future held. Simeon, under God's direction, opened Mary's eyes to some of the suffering Jesus would face when he declared that "many will oppose him."

At this time, Mary didn't know that many would despise Jesus, or that an angry mob would nail her son to a cross and she'd watch as he died. Even as a sword pierced Jesus' side, pain would pierce Mary's heart. As she stood at the foot of the Cross, did Mary think of Simeon's prophecy given over thirty years earlier?

Jesus chose to die for our sins so we can spend eternity in heaven, but the joy of salvation and the pain of the Cross are inseparable. Mary watched in agony as Jesus died, but joy came to her later when she learned that he had risen from the dead.

When the angel first gave Mary the news that God had chosen her, she knew it wasn't going to be an easy life, but she agreed to it, not knowing what was ahead. And because of that she had a privilege no one else has ever had—to be the earthly mother of our Lord.

Pray: Thank Jesus for enduring the agony of the Cross and being with you in your own suffering.

> Simeon blessed them, and he said to Mary, the baby's mother,
> "This child is destined to cause many in Israel to fall, and
> many others to rise. He has been sent as a sign from God,
> but many will oppose him. As a result, the deepest thoughts
> of many hearts will be revealed. And a sword will pierce your
> very soul."
> LUKE 2:34-35

Puzzle Page

S imeon told Mary that she would experience deep sadness. Solve the Telephone Puzzle to decode the verse about dealing with hard times.

Directions: This puzzle has two numbers under each blank. The first number matches one of the phone buttons. The second number tells you which letter on the button to write down. For instance, "9.3" means letter 3 on button 9. Check your answer below.

___ ___ ___ ___ ___ ___ be
2.1 5.3 9.1 2.1 9.3 7.4

___ ___ ___ ___ ___ ___.
5.1 6.3 9.3 3.3 8.2 5.3

___ ___ ___ ___ ___ stop
6.2 3.2 8.3 3.2 7.3

___ ___ ___ ___ ___ ___ ___.
7.1 7.3 2.1 9.3 4.3 6.2 4.1

Be ___ ___ ___ ___ ___ ___ ___ ___ in all
8.1 4.2 2.1 6.2 5.2 3.3 8.2 5.3

___ ___ ___ ___ ___ ___ ___ ___ ___ ___ ___ ___ ___ ,
2.3 4.3 7.3 2.3 8.2 6.1 7.4 8.1 2.1 6.2 2.3 3.2 7.4

for this is ___ ___ ___ ' ___ ___ ___ ___ ___ for
4.1 6.3 3.1 7.4 9.1 4.3 5.3 5.3

___ ___ ___ ___ ___ ___ ___ ___ ___ ___ ___ to
9.3 6.3 8.2 9.1 4.2 6.3 2.2 3.2 5.3 6.3 6.2 4.1

___ ___ ___ ___ ___ ___ ___ ___ ___ ___.
2.3 4.2 7.3 4.3 7.4 8.1 5.1 3.2 7.4 8.2 7.4

Phone buttons		
1	2 ABC	3 DEF
4 GHI	5 JKL	6 MNO
7 PQRS	8 TUV	9 WXYZ
*	0 OPER	#

Journey to Safety

Read about Jesus' family escaping to Egypt in Matthew 2:13-23.

God put a special star in the sky to alert the wise men that the new King had been born. They traveled a long distance and then stopped to ask King Herod where to find the new King. This made Herod angry and jealous. God warned the wise men in a dream not to return to Herod, so they went home a different way. When Herod realized the wise men were not going to return to tell him where to find the young King, he became even angrier. He decided to kill all the baby boys in Bethlehem who were the right age to be the child the wise men had inquired about.

An angel appeared to Joseph and told him to escape with Mary and Jesus to Egypt. Sadness and grieving filled the land as families lost their precious sons, but the Messiah was kept safe. The holy family stayed in Egypt until Herod died. Then they returned to Nazareth.

Mary must have been a very courageous young woman to handle all that happened to her in such a short amount of time. She was a young virgin chosen to give birth to the Messiah. She made a long journey just when her baby was due, delivered her infant in a stable, and then had to flee to Egypt. Mary wasn't alone, though. Joseph was with her, and God knew Joseph would take good care of Mary and baby Jesus. God himself was also with Mary, giving her the strength and courage to face the things she encountered.

When God gives someone a job to do, he gives her people who can guide and help her, and he is with her too.

Pray: Ask God to give you the courage to face the hard things in your life in a way that honors him.

> After the wise men were gone, an angel of the Lord appeared to Joseph in a dream. "Get up! Flee to Egypt with the child and his mother," the angel said. "Stay there until I tell you to return, because Herod is going to search for the child to kill him."
> MATTHEW 2:13

Say Yes to God

Read about how God is all you need in Philippians 4:11-13.

God can use anyone who is willing, but that doesn't mean he'll always call you to do easy things. It doesn't work that way. God may call you to do some difficult tasks, but he will give you what you need to succeed.

Just imagine how some of the Bible women felt when God gave them a task to do. What did Rebekah think about as she traveled farther and farther from home and everything she knew? Was she afraid, or did she dream about Isaac and wonder if she would find true love? God gave her the courage and strength she needed to leave everything behind and make the long journey to her future.

The widow of Zarephath was sure she and her son were going to starve when Elijah asked her to feed him. She had no guarantee his promise of unlimited oil and flour throughout the famine was true. She didn't even worship the true God at this point, yet God chose her to feed his prophet.

Mary agreed to give birth to God's son, even though other people wouldn't understand why she was pregnant. She risked Joseph assuming she had been with another man and not wanting to marry her anymore. She was willing to do whatever God asked of her, even if it seemed impossible. She called herself a servant of the Lord.

Do you have the same attitude? Are you ready to do whatever God asks of you?

God may call you to do something hard, but he'll give you the courage, wisdom, and ability to do it just as he did for the women of the Bible. Don't miss out on the adventure by being afraid to say yes to God.

Pray: Tell God that you want to say yes to him.

> And I heard the voice of the Lord saying, "Whom shall I send, and who will go for us?" Then I said, "Here I am! Send me."
> ISAIAH 6:8, ESV

Puzzle Page

*M*any women in the Bible did amazing things with God's help. Decode the Thermometer Puzzle below to find out what the Bible says about seeking God.

Directions: Look at the thermometer. Each temperature has a corresponding letter. Look at the temperatures under the lines below. Above each line, write the letter that goes with the temperature. Check your answers below.

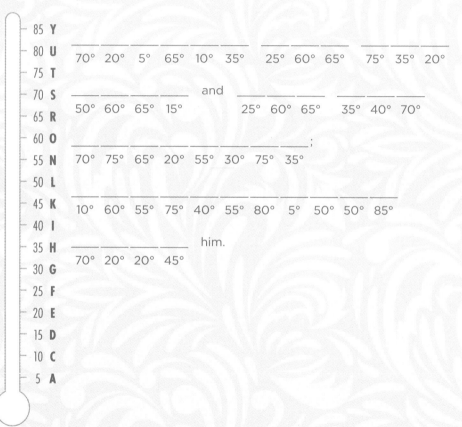

85 Y
80 U
75 T
70 S
65 R
60 O
55 N
50 L
45 K
40 I
35 H
30 G
25 F
20 E
15 D
10 C
5 A

_____ _____ _____ _____ _____ _____   _____ _____ _____   _____ _____ _____
70° 20° 5° 65° 10° 35°   25° 60° 65°   75° 35° 20°

_____ _____ _____ _____   and   _____ _____ _____   _____ _____ _____
50° 60° 65° 15°   25° 60° 65°   35° 40° 70°

_____ _____ _____ _____ _____ _____ _____ _____ ;
70° 75° 65° 20° 55° 30° 75° 35°

_____ _____ _____ _____ _____ _____ _____ _____ _____ _____ _____
10° 60° 55° 75° 40° 55° 80° 5° 50° 50° 85°

_____ _____ _____ _____   him.
70° 20° 20° 45°

Jesus Sees

Read about the Samaritan woman meeting Jesus at the well in John 4:1-26.

One day Jesus was traveling with his disciples, and they stopped along the road in Samaria. Jesus sat by a well while his disciples went into town to find food. A woman came to draw water. Most women drew their water early in the morning or in the evening when it was cooler. This nameless woman may have chosen to come at noontime to avoid the other women, who probably gossiped about her sinful lifestyle.

When she arrived at the well, Jesus spoke to her and asked for water. This surprised the woman. Jesus told her, "If you only knew the gift God has for you and who you are speaking to, you would ask me, and I would give you living water" (John 4:10). Jesus meant he could fill her inner longing. He saw her true need—forgiveness and a cleansed heart.

Jesus knew she didn't have a husband, yet he told her to go get her husband. He was testing her to see what she would say. Jesus knew her heart. He knew her sin. Best of all, he alone had the cure for her sin.

The conversation continued, and the woman said she knew the Messiah would come. Then Jesus did something he didn't normally do. He told her, "I AM the Messiah!" (John 4:26). And because he is the Messiah, he was able to offer her the forgiveness she needed.

Jesus sees your heart and knows your needs. If you haven't accepted his gift of forgiveness, don't put it off. Talk to God and a trusted adult about it today.

Pray: Thank God for seeing your heart and forgiving your sins.

> Jesus replied, "Anyone who drinks this water will soon become thirsty again. But those who drink the water I give will never be thirsty again. It becomes a fresh, bubbling spring within them, giving them eternal life."
> JOHN 4:13-14

Bringing Others to Jesus

Read about the Samaritan woman sharing her faith in John 4:39-42.

*J*esus revealed to the woman at the well that he was the Messiah. The woman left her water jar there and ran back to the village with the news. Most of the people knew her story and normally shunned her. They were probably astonished to see her running to the village, talking excitedly about a Jewish man she'd met at the well.

The woman's excitement was contagious, and the people flocked to the well to meet Jesus. There isn't a record of what Jesus said to the people, but we can assume that he spoke to them of God and the laws they already knew. He probably shared the same things with them that he'd shared with the woman about salvation and worshiping God. The people may have been filled with questions, and Jesus would have patiently answered them. The Samaritans were so open to the gospel that Jesus stayed for two days talking to them.

Many of the people in the Samaritan village of Sychar believed in Jesus during those two days. The entire village was changed by Jesus' visit, and it began with a woman considered an outcast by her neighbors. She was probably the least likely prospect to become a believer in Jesus, yet she is the one Jesus approached. Her heart was receptive to the message, perhaps because she realized she was a sinner and in need of a Savior. If Jesus had approached a more religious person, he or she may not have seen the need for a Savior.

When we share the gospel, we often avoid people who look less open to it. Yet we never know who most needs to hear Jesus' message.

Be bold and ready to share your faith with whomever God brings to you.

Pray: Talk to God about someone in your life with whom you want to share the gospel and ask him for an opportunity to do so.

> The woman left her water jar beside the well and ran back to the village, telling everyone, "Come and see a man who told me everything I ever did! Could he possibly be the Messiah?"
> JOHN 4:28-29

Puzzle Page

Solve the Telephone Puzzle below to find out how you can be a witness for Jesus.

Directions: This puzzle has two numbers under each blank. The first number matches one of the phone buttons. The second number tells you which letter on the button to write down. For instance, "9.3" means letter 3 on button 9. Check your answer below.

For ____ ____ ____   ____ ____ ____ to be
    9.3 6.3 8.2   2.1 7.3 3.2

____ ____ ____   ____ ____ ____ ____ ____ ____ ____,
4.2 4.3 7.4   9.1 4.3 8.1 6.2 3.2 7.4 7.4

____ ____ ____ ____ ____ ____ ____
8.1 3.2 5.3 5.3 4.3 6.2 4.1

____ ____ ____ ____ ____ ____ ____ ____ what
3.2 8.3 3.2 7.3 9.3 6.3 6.2 3.2

you ____ ____ ____ ____   ____ ____ ____ ____
    4.2 2.1 8.3 3.2   7.4 3.2 3.2 6.2

and ____ ____ ____ ____ ____.
    4.2 3.2 2.1 7.3 3.1

1	2 ABC	3 DEF
4 GHI	5 JKL	6 MNO
7 PQRS	8 TUV	9 WXYZ
*	0 OPER	#

Healed by Faith

Read about the woman who bravely touched Jesus' robe in Mark 5:24-34.

While Jesus was making his way to the home of a very sick young girl, a crowd surrounded him. In the crowd was a woman who had been bleeding for twelve years. She'd gone to several doctors, but they hadn't helped her. Her hope was gone. Then she heard Jesus could heal people.

The woman joined the crowd that thronged Jesus. Her plan was to touch his robe in hopes that his healing power would cure her. With that purpose in mind, she inched forward until she was able to reach out and touch his garment. As soon as she did, she felt the bleeding stop, and she was immediately well. Imagine her relief after having lived with her infirmity for twelve years. She didn't have to take medicine for weeks or have repeated follow-up visits. She was able to do all the things she hadn't been able to do for many years as her condition made her weaker and weaker with each passing day.

When Jesus felt the healing power go out from him, he asked, "Who touched my robe?" (Mark 5:30).

The disciples thought this was a strange question. With so many people crowding around him, how could anyone know who it was? They didn't realize someone had been healed by touching his garment.

The woman dropped to her knees in front of Jesus and told him what had happened. Perhaps she was worried Jesus would be angry or he'd cause her illness to return, but Jesus told her, "Daughter, your faith has made you well. Go in peace. Your suffering is over" (Mark 5:34). The woman was overjoyed. She knew she really was restored to health.

This woman was healed because of her faith in Jesus. Your faith can heal you as well.

Pray: Ask Jesus to heal any parts of your life that feel broken or hurt.

> She had heard about Jesus, so she came up behind him through the crowd and touched his robe. For she thought to herself, "If I can just touch his robe, I will be healed."
> MARK 5:27-28

God Looks at the Heart

Read about the widow's generous offering in Mark 12:41-44.

*J*esus was watching as many rich people filed past the Temple donation box and put in generous offerings. Then a poor widow walked by the box and dropped in two small coins.

Jesus called his disciples over and told them that he was more pleased by the woman's offering than that of the rich men. He told them that the woman had given more than all the others. The disciples looked at him in surprise. How could she have given more than all the rich men?

But of course Jesus wasn't talking about the actual amount; he meant she had given all she had—compared to the wealthy people, who gave only a small percentage of their money.

God doesn't really need anyone's money. He created everything, and he owns everything. We are just caretakers of his money. But the rich people didn't view it that way. They were proud of their wealth, and they wanted everyone to see their big offerings. Other people might have been impressed, but Jesus wasn't.

Jesus saw the hearts of those who gave their offerings. The attitude of a person's heart is much more important to Jesus than his or her appearance. Jesus didn't like what he saw in the rich men's hearts. They were contributing large offerings for show, but they didn't really sacrifice anything to give to God. But Jesus saw the poor woman's heart and knew she was making a big sacrifice to give her two small coins.

Jesus sees your heart too. Are you cultivating a heart that is generous and willing to give? Or are you holding too tightly to money and possessions?

Pray: Ask God to make you unafraid to give generously back to him.

> The LORD doesn't see things the way you see them. People judge by outward appearance, but the LORD looks at the heart.
> 1 SAMUEL 16:7

Puzzle Page

$\mathcal{G}$od wants you to give generously, just like the woman at the Temple. Solve the Balloon Puzzle to find out God's promise for you when you give.

Directions: Each balloon has both a scrambled word and a number in it. There are also numbers next to the blank spots in the verse. Look at the number next to each blank. Find the balloon with the same number. Unscramble the word in that balloon, and write it in the blank. Check your answers at the bottom.

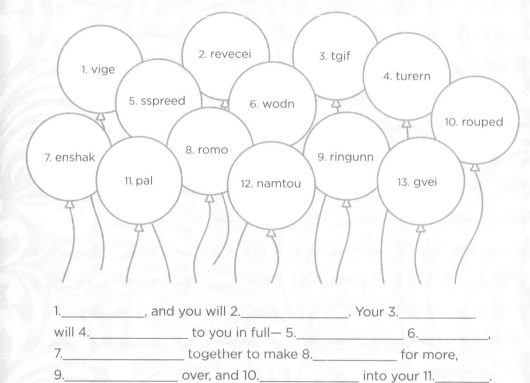

1. vige
2. revecei
3. tgif
4. turern
5. sspreed
6. wodn
7. enshak
8. romo
9. ringunn
10. rouped
11. pal
12. namtou
13. gvei

1._____, and you will 2._____. Your 3._____ will 4._____ to you in full— 5._____ 6._____, 7._____ together to make 8._____ for more, 9._____ over, and 10._____ into your 11._____. The 12._____ you 13._____ will determine the 12._____ you get back.

Do you think this verse was just for the people Jesus was talking to at the time or for us today too? Why?

Bold Repentance

Read about the woman who anointed Jesus with oil in Luke 7:36-50.

Simon the Pharisee was upset when a known sinner showed up uninvited at his dinner. This woman approached Jesus weeping. She knew she was guilty of sin and that he was able to help her. Her tears fell on Jesus' dusty feet, and she wiped his feet with her hair. She kissed his feet and then opened a small alabaster container holding precious perfume and poured it over his feet. Only a small drop was needed for fragrance, but she poured out her whole container.

Simon didn't say anything aloud, but he was thinking that if Jesus were really a prophet, he would know the woman was a sinner. Jesus knew what Simon was thinking and answered his thoughts. He asked Simon a question: A man loaned one person five hundred pieces of silver and another fifty pieces, but neither could repay him. The man canceled both debts. Who would love the man more? Simon correctly chose the man who had the greater debt canceled.

Jesus told Simon, "Her sins—and they are many—have been forgiven, so she has shown me much love. But a person who is forgiven little shows only little love" (Luke 7:47). The woman's bold repentance led her to the feet of Jesus. She knew that she needed help, and she wasn't concerned about crashing a party and making an emotional scene to get it. In Jesus, the woman found forgiveness and healing for her troubled heart.

If your heart doesn't feel at peace today, there may be something you need to talk to God about. Once you confess your sins and ask for his forgiveness, you'll experience peace and healing in your heart.

Pray: Confess your sins and receive God's abundant mercy and forgiveness.

Search me, O God, and know my heart; test me and know my anxious thoughts. Point out anything in me that offends you, and lead me along the path of everlasting life.
PSALM 139:23-24

A Changed Life

Read about Mary Magdalene deciding to follow Jesus in Luke 8:1-3.

*W*hen Mary met Jesus, everything changed. Mary didn't return to her home in Magdala after she met Jesus; she traveled with him and his twelve disciples and some other women. Perhaps Mary felt if she returned home, everyone would remember her as the woman who'd been possessed by demons. They knew her as a wild-eyed madwoman. Or maybe Mary wanted to stay close to Jesus to make sure the demons didn't return. Or she may have just followed him out of love for her Savior. That love wouldn't let her turn back or return to her old home.

Not only did Mary leave everything behind to follow Jesus, but she helped support his ministry financially. Jesus and the disciples left their jobs behind. They didn't have any worldly possessions. They needed to eat and have a place to stay while they traveled and ministered. Mary willingly gave her money to support the Lord's work.

When you accept Jesus as your Savior, your life changes. Mary's changed more than most, but every person's life should be transformed when he or she meets the Savior. Love and gratitude for salvation moved Mary to support her Lord and to follow him to the end. Love and gratitude for salvation should do the same for each person who calls Jesus his or her Savior.

Hopefully you can clearly see how your faith in Jesus makes a difference in your life. If not, let Jesus change your heart and actively seek to do his will.

Pray: Ask Jesus to make you more like him every day.

> This means that anyone who belongs to Christ has become a new person. The old life is gone; a new life has begun!
> 2 CORINTHIANS 5:17

Puzzle Page

*M*ary Magdalene and the woman who anointed Jesus both found the forgiveness they needed. Solve the Telephone Puzzle to read what the Bible says about God's mercy.

Directions: This puzzle has two numbers under each blank. The first number matches one of the phone buttons. The second number tells you which letter on the button to write down. For instance, "9.3" means letter 3 on button 9. Check your answer below.

___ ___ ___ ___ ___ ___ who
7.1 3.2 6.3 7.1 5.3 3.2

___ ___ ___ ___ ___ ___ ___ their
2.3 6.3 6.2 2.3 3.2 2.1 5.3

___ ___ ___ ___ will not
7.4 4.3 6.2 7.4

___ ___ ___ ___ ___ ___ ___ ,
7.1 7.3 6.3 7.4 7.1 3.2 7.3

but if they ___ ___ ___ ___ ___ ___ ___ and ___ ___ ___ ___
2.3 6.3 6.2 3.3 3.2 7.4 7.4   8.1 8.2 7.3 6.2

from ___ ___ ___ ___ , ___ ___ ___ ___ will
8.1 4.2 3.2 6.1   8.1 4.2 3.2 9.3

___ ___ ___ ___ ___ ___ ___   ___ ___ ___ ___ ___ .
7.3 3.2 2.3 3.2 4.3 8.3 3.2   6.1 3.2 7.3 2.3 9.3

1	**2** ABC	**3** DEF
4 GHI	**5** JKL	**6** MNO
7 PQRS	**8** TUV	**9** WXYZ
*	**0** OPER	#

The Sisters' Belief

Read about the miracle Mary and Martha witnessed in John 11:1-44.

Mary and Martha were worried. Their brother, Lazarus, was very sick. The sisters sent a messenger to Jesus asking him to come. Jesus waited a couple of days, even though he knew Lazarus would die while he was away.

Jesus and his disciples went to Bethany, where Mary and Martha lived. Martha went out to meet him, while Mary waited in the house. Martha said, "Lord, if only you had been here, my brother would not have died. But even now I know that God will give you whatever you ask" (verses 21-22).

Jesus told Martha that Lazarus would rise again. Martha said, "Yes . . . he will rise when everyone else rises, at the last day" (verse 24).

But Jesus meant he was going to bring Lazarus back to life right then. Jesus said, "I am the resurrection and the life. Anyone who believes in me will live, even after dying. Everyone who lives in me and believes in me will never ever die" (verses 25-26).

Martha believed this. She and Mary knew that Jesus was the Son of God. Mary and Martha showed Jesus where Lazarus was buried. Jesus ordered the stone moved aside. He prayed, and then he shouted, "Lazarus, come out!" (verse 43). Jesus wanted everyone to hear and believe.

Lazarus walked out of the tomb, still wrapped in his grave clothes. Many people believed in Jesus when this happened.

Before Lazarus was raised, Martha believed that Jesus was the Messiah and that he could help her, but she had no idea what he was going to do for her family that day. Even if we believe in Jesus, we don't always realize the extent of his power and love. Jesus can raise the dead, and he can help you through your difficulties in ways you can't even imagine.

Pray: Thank Jesus for his love and his gift of everlasting life.

> "Yes, Lord," [Martha] told him. "I have always believed you are the Messiah, the Son of God, the one who has come into the world from God."
> JOHN 11:27

A Selfless Gift

Read about Mary anointing Jesus in John 12:1-11.

*T*here is some confusion about this story of Mary anointing Jesus with oil. It's very similar to the story of the woman who anointed Jesus in Luke 7 (whom you read about earlier in this book). Sometimes people think it's the same story, and that Mary is that woman, but that's not true.

In this story, it was just a few days before the Passover celebration was to begin. Jesus had raised Lazarus from the dead, and he was at Mary, Martha, and Lazarus's home, where they were having a special dinner in his honor.

Mary took a twelve-ounce jar of expensive perfume and anointed Jesus' feet with it, then wiped them with her hair. The fragrance filled the whole house. Judas, who later betrayed Jesus, immediately criticized Mary. "That perfume was worth a year's wages. It should have been sold and the money given to the poor" (John 12:5). Judas didn't really care about the poor; he only cared about money. He was in charge of the disciples' money and often stole from it.

Jesus was quick to defend her: "Leave her alone. She did this in preparation for my burial. You will always have the poor among you, but you will not always have me" (John 12:7-8). Mary showed a spiritual sensitivity beyond what the others displayed. She honored Jesus by anointing him with perfume worth a year's pay. Some considered it a waste, but not Mary—and not Jesus.

Different people have different ways of honoring God today. Some do it through gifts of money, others through acts of service. What's important to God is the person's heart attitude. Mary's act was an unselfish one motivated by love, and ours should be also.

Pray: Ask God to shape your heart to be humble and generous.

> Mary took a twelve-ounce jar of expensive perfume made from essence of nard, and she anointed Jesus' feet with it, wiping his feet with her hair. The house was filled with the fragrance.
> JOHN 12:3

Puzzle Page

Sometimes we let life's problems and disappointments get us down. What should we do instead? Solve the Balloon Puzzle to find out.

Directions: Each balloon has both a scrambled word and a number in it. There are also numbers next to the blank spots in the verse. Look at the number next to each blank. Find the balloon with the same number. Unscramble the word in that balloon, and write it in the blank. Check your answers at the bottom.

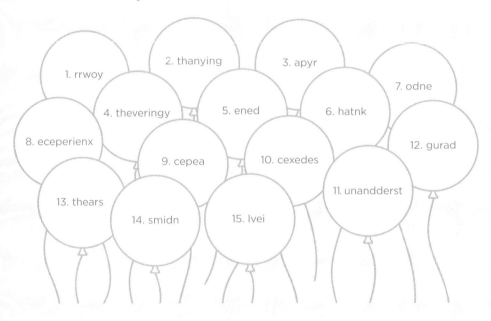

1. rrwoy
2. thanying
3. apyr
4. theveringy
5. ened
6. hatnk
7. odne
8. eceperienx
9. cepea
10. cexedes
11. unandderst
12. gurad
13. thears
14. smidn
15. lvei

Don't 1._____ about 2._____; instead, 3._____ about 4. _____. Tell God what you 5._____, and 6._____ him for all he has 7. _____. Then you will 8._____ God's 9._____, which 10._____ anything we can 11._____. His 9._____ will 12._____ your 13._____ and 14._____ as you 15._____ in Christ Jesus.

What can you do today when problems get you down?

The Women Who Followed Jesus

Read about Mary Magdalene's loyalty during Jesus' crucifixion and burial in Mark 15:33-41.

Mary Magdalene and several other women followed Jesus throughout his ministry. They traveled with him and helped support him financially.

These brave women didn't leave Jesus and return home when things got tough. They remained with Jesus as the religious leaders cried out against him. They stayed nearby as he was sentenced to death. They followed as he made the walk to Calvary, where he was crucified. They were there even after other followers fled.

The women who loved Jesus, many of whom he had healed from illnesses or delivered from bondage to demons, watched for six hours as Jesus hung on the Cross and died.

They must have been filled with grief. Jesus had totally changed their lives. They knew who he truly was. They were devoted followers and stood together near the one they loved.

Even after Jesus died and everyone else left, Mary Magdalene and another woman named Mary stayed. They followed as Jesus' body was taken down, prepared for burial, and then laid in a tomb.

Mary Magdalene stayed at Jesus' tomb for as long as she could before having to leave to observe the Sabbath. This must have been the saddest Sabbath she had ever kept. But her sadness would soon be turned to joy.

Pray: Ask Jesus to help you become completely devoted to him.

> Some women were there, watching from a distance, including Mary Magdalene, Mary (the mother of James the younger and of Joseph), and Salome. They had been followers of Jesus and had cared for him while he was in Galilee. Many other women who had come with him to Jerusalem were also there.
>
> MARK 15:40-41

Seeing the Risen Lord

Read about Mary Magdalene seeing the resurrected Jesus in John 20:1-18.

*T*he Sabbath was over, and Mary Magdalene, filled with sorrow, made her way to Jesus' tomb. What a surprise awaited her there! The large stone covering the entrance was rolled away, and the tomb was empty. She ran back to Jerusalem and told Peter and John that Jesus had risen. The men raced to the tomb to see for themselves, then left.

Mary Magdalene stayed to grieve. She was crying alone at the tomb when she had a privilege no one else got. She was the first to see the risen Lord. Initially, she thought he was the gardener. But when Jesus said her name, she recognized him.

It's interesting that Jesus didn't appear first to some of his twelve disciples or to his own mother. Instead he chose Mary Magdalene, a faithful follower ever since Jesus delivered her from demon possession. Why did she get this privilege? Perhaps because her devotion was greatest. Jesus called the twelve disciples to follow him, and God chose Mary to be his mother, but Mary Magdalene followed Jesus out of love and gratitude.

With one word—her name, "Mary"—her world was made right again. Her Savior was alive. Death hadn't conquered him. He'd defeated death and sin.

Jesus called Mary by name, and he calls you by name too. Jesus knows all about you—your needs, your desires, your hopes, and your plans. You can't see him physically as Mary Magdalene did, but you can see his work in your life, hear his voice as he speaks to your heart through his Word, and be filled with his peace as you leave your worries with him.

Pray: Praise Jesus for defeating death and giving you hope in him.

> You have turned my mourning into joyful dancing. You have taken away my clothes of mourning and clothed me with joy, that I might sing praises to you and not be silent. O Lord my God, I will give you thanks forever!
> PSALM 30:11-12

Puzzle Page

*B*ecause of Jesus' death and resurrection, you can be forgiven of your sins and have hope for the future. Solve the Speedometer Puzzle below to read a verse about hope.

Directions: Each blank line has a number under it. Those numbers correspond to a letter on the speedometer. Decode the words and check your answer below.

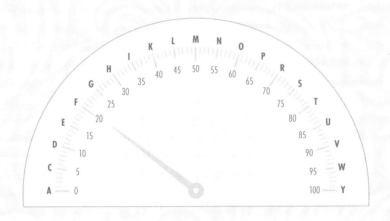

But if we _____ _____ to
          45 60 60 40   20 60 70 95 0 70 10

_____ we _____ '___
75 60 50 15 80 30 35 55 25   10 60 55 80

yet _____, we must _____
    30 0 90 15   95 0 35 80

_____ and
65 0 80 35 15 55 80 45 100

_____.
5 60 55 20 35 10 15 55 80 45 100

Telling the Good News

Read Jesus' command to tell others about him in Matthew 28:16-20.

After Jesus appeared to Mary Magdalene, he told her to tell his disciples he was going to his Father. Mary took the message to Jesus' followers. She probably repeated the story over and over as each of them questioned her. And she probably continued telling the story of her resurrected Lord for the rest of her life. He'd made such a change in her, and she'd been the first one to see him after he rose from the dead. That was something worth sharing.

When Jesus changes someone's life in such a dramatic way, it's only natural they tell others about it. Remember the Samaritan woman at the well? She ran and told the townspeople about her meeting with Jesus. She got them to return to the well to hear Jesus for themselves.

Jesus wants us to tell others about our encounter with him too. We don't talk with him face-to-face as the Samaritan woman and Mary Magdalene did. But in a spiritual sense, all of us who claim him as Savior do come face-to-face with him, and one day we will see him personally in heaven. In the meantime, he has appointed us to take the gospel to those around us.

Mary Magdalene wasn't a preacher or evangelist; she was just a woman sharing what she'd seen and experienced. That's the best way to communicate the Good News of salvation. Has Jesus changed your life? Have you experienced his forgiveness? Simply tell others how you met Jesus and what he's done for you. If you can't think of anything to say, you may not be paying attention to God's work in your life.

Keep your testimony fresh as you open yourself to what God wants for you, and grow in your faith by daily reading God's Word, praying, and seeking to follow God's plan. If you do those things, you'll always have something to share with others about the difference Jesus makes in your life.

Pray: Ask Jesus for the courage to share your faith with others.

Mary Magdalene found the disciples and told them, "I have seen the Lord!" Then she gave them his message.
JOHN 20:18

Sharing the Gospel

Read about Lydia putting her faith in Jesus and sharing the gospel with her household in Acts 16:13-15.

*L*ydia was a wealthy and influential woman in Philippi. She was originally from Thyatira, a city famous for its purple dye. The dye was hard to produce, so it was expensive, as was the purple fabric made from it. Lydia made a good living selling it.

Philippi was a thriving Roman colony without enough Jewish men to have a synagogue. Jewish law said there must be ten men to form a synagogue, but the women could meet together to pray without a formal place.

A group of Jewish women met at the riverside to pray. The Bible doesn't say if Lydia was Jewish or a Gentile who joined them, but many think she was a Gentile who was seeking God.

God sent Paul and his traveling companions, Silas, Timothy, and Luke, to Philippi, where they found the group of women. Paul shared with them how Jesus, God's Son, had come to earth, how he was crucified, rose again, and now lives in heaven. Paul told the women they could be saved from their sins by believing in Jesus. Lydia became a believer that day. And as she shared what she'd learned, the other members of her household became believers too. Lydia may have been a widow, and the others in her household were perhaps her grown children or servants. The Bible doesn't say. The important thing is that, once Lydia was a believer, she shared the gospel with them.

God wants you to get excited about your faith and take the gospel everywhere you go. You can share about Jesus at your gymnastics class, soccer practice, dance rehearsal, honor club, science class, drama club, neighborhood pool, and family dinner table. If you encounter challenges, don't give up. Ask God to show you the best way to reach your family and friends for him.

Pray: Ask God to build in you the desire and courage to enthusiastically share the gospel wherever you go.

> One of them was Lydia from Thyatira, a merchant of expensive purple cloth, who worshiped God. As she listened to us, the Lord opened her heart, and she accepted what Paul was saying.
> ACTS 16:14

Puzzle Page

We should always be ready to share our Christian faith, just like Mary Magdalene and Lydia were. Solve the Balloon Puzzle to find out what the Bible says about sharing our faith.

Directions: Each balloon has both a scrambled word and a number in it. There are also numbers next to the blank spots in the verse. Look at the number next to each blank. Find the balloon with the same number. Unscramble the word in that balloon, and write it in the blank. Check your answers at the bottom.

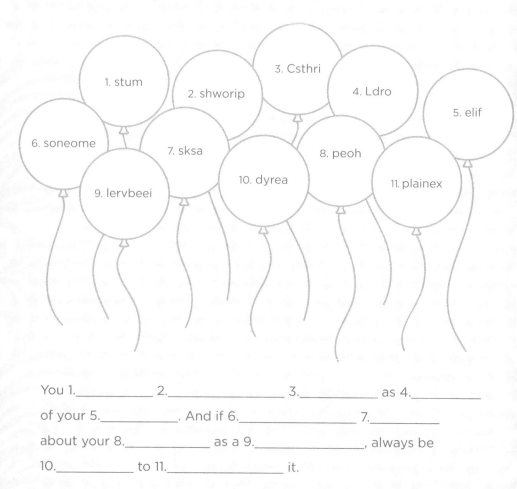

1. stum
2. shworip
3. Csthri
4. Ldro
5. elif
6. soneome
7. sksa
8. peoh
9. lervbeei
10. dyrea
11. plainex

You 1._____ 2._____ 3._____ as 4._____ of your 5._____. And if 6._____ 7._____ about your 8._____ as a 9._____, always be 10._____ to 11._____ it.

The Beginning of a Church

Read about Paul and Silas returning to Lydia's home after being released from prison in Acts 16:16-40.

After Lydia became a believer, she asked Paul and his mission team—Silas, Timothy, and Luke, and possibly more—to stay at her house. Lydia wasn't afraid to take the risk of hosting believers in her home.

One day the mission team met a slave girl possessed by a demon. She earned a lot of money for her master by telling fortunes. She followed Paul and the others, shouting, "These men are servants of the Most High God, and they have come to tell you how to be saved" (Acts 16:17).

Finally Paul turned to the girl and said to the demon within her, "I command you in the name of Jesus Christ to come out of her" (verse 18). The demon left the girl, and she was no longer able to tell fortunes—or make money for her master. This made the master angry. He dragged Paul and Silas into the marketplace and turned a mob against them. They were beaten and thrown into prison.

But even though they were behind bars and in pain from the beating, Paul and Silas prayed and sang songs to God. Around midnight there was an earthquake; the whole jail shook, and the prisoners were freed. The guard knew he'd be blamed for the prisoners' escape, so he got out his sword to kill himself. Paul said, "Stop! Don't kill yourself! We are all here!" (verse 28). He shared the gospel with the man and his family, and they all became believers that night.

Then Paul and Silas returned to Lydia's house, where the believers were gathered. Because Lydia believed and was willing to open her home, she hosted the beginnings of the church at Philippi.

Sometimes we take churches for granted. What can you do to show appreciation for your church? Instead of just attending church this month, see what you can contribute.

Pray: Thank God for your church.

> When Paul and Silas left the prison, they returned to the home of Lydia. There they met with the believers and encouraged them once more. Then they left town.
> ACTS 16:40

Influencing Others

Read about Lois and Eunice's godly influence in 2 Timothy 1:3-7.

*L*ois and Eunice are known for being Timothy's grandmother and mother. We first meet Eunice in Acts 16 when Paul asks Timothy to accompany him on a missionary trip. Timothy's mother isn't mentioned by name there, but we're told she was a Jewish believer, and his father was Greek.

Lois and Eunice were familiar with the Old Testament Scriptures, and they taught these to Timothy from the time he was a very young child. Timothy was an eager learner, and he loved God. But even though Lois, Eunice, and Timothy loved God and the Scriptures, they didn't know about Jesus. They probably became believers in Jesus when Paul traveled through their city of Lystra, in the hill country of present-day Turkey, on an earlier trip.

Lois and Eunice went about their daily work of cooking, cleaning, and raising Timothy. They were just living out their lives, but they were also leaving a legacy of faith that started with Lois and passed to Eunice and then to Timothy.

Lois and Eunice influenced Timothy while they raised him, but *you* influence people too without even knowing it. Every time you tell someone about Jesus, you plant a seed in her heart. When you say a kind word to a classmate, you brighten her day. When you take a few minutes to help a sibling with a chore, you encourage him or her. Every time you smile at a cashier or a stranger you pass in the mall, you make a difference.

The more time you invest in someone, the more you influence her. If you want to make a difference in a friend's or sibling's life, shower her with kindness every day. Don't be afraid to share what you learn in your daily Bible reading. Listen as she talks and offer godly advice. You never know what difference you may make in someone's life.

Pray: Ask God to help you point others to him.

> I remember your genuine faith, for you share the faith that first filled your grandmother Lois and your mother, Eunice. And I know that same faith continues strong in you.
> 2 TIMOTHY 1:5

Puzzle Page

*L*ydia, Lois, and Eunice encouraged others in their faith. Solve the Balloon Puzzle below to find out what the Bible says about caring for other Christians.

Directions: Each balloon has both a scrambled word and a number in it. There are also numbers next to the blank spots in the verse. Look at the number next to each blank. Find the balloon with the same number. Unscramble the word in that balloon, and write it in the blank. Check your answers at the bottom.

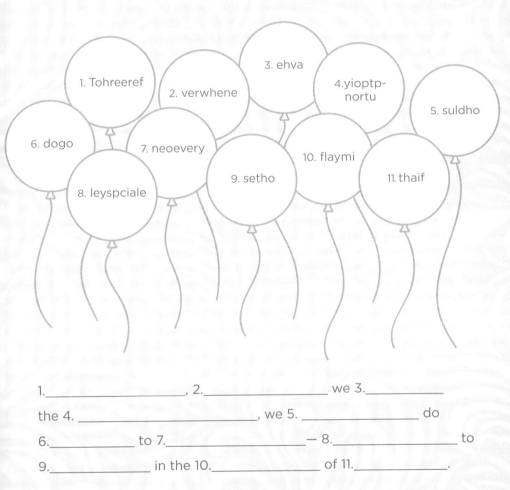

1. Tohreeref
2. verwhene
3. ehva
4. yioptp-nortu
5. suldho
6. dogo
7. neoevery
8. leyspciale
9. setho
10. flaymi
11. thaif

1._____, 2._____ we 3._____
the 4. _____, we 5. _____ do
6._____ to 7._____ — 8._____ to
9._____ in the 10._____ of 11._____.

Serving God Together

Read about the ministry of Priscilla and her husband, Aquila, in Acts 18:1-28.

*I*n Scripture, Priscilla and Aquila are always mentioned together. They are one of many sets of names we've come to know as Bible spouses—Adam and Eve, Abraham and Sarah, Mary and Joseph. When both spouses love and honor God, they can accomplish a lot together for the Lord.

Priscilla and Aquila were tentmakers and valuable coworkers of Paul. After hosting Paul for a year and a half in their Corinth home, the couple went to Ephesus with him. Paul left them there to establish a church in their home. During their ministry, the couple met Apollos, who was enthusiastic in his teaching but didn't know the whole gospel. He was still waiting for the promised Messiah. The couple took him in and told him about salvation through Christ. They taught him all the things they had learned, and Apollos went on to preach about Jesus.

Priscilla and Aquila went back to Rome, and soon a church was meeting in their house there. They eventually moved back to Ephesus, possibly to avoid persecution in Rome. Throughout all their travels, ministry, and church planting, Priscilla and Aquila maintained their tentmaking trade and continued to serve Jesus.

God uses couples who are willing to serve him together. That's why it's important to be discerning about who you date, and especially who you marry. As you start thinking about your future, ask God to ignite a passion in your heart to serve him and only date a guy who is dedicated to serving God alongside you.

Pray: Tell God that you want to serve him with your future.

Give my greetings to Priscilla and Aquila, my coworkers in the ministry of Christ Jesus. In fact, they once risked their lives for me. I am thankful to them, and so are all the Gentile churches. Also give my greetings to the church that meets in their home.
ROMANS 16:3-5

Brave Women

Read about holding tightly to your hope in Jesus in Hebrews 10:23-25.

Many women in the Bible followed Jesus despite the risks. Mary Magdalene traveled with Jesus. She and Jesus' mother followed him all the way to the Cross. While some of the disciples fled, the women stayed. They were among the first to find out Jesus had risen.

After Jesus died, rose from the dead, and ascended into heaven, the people who hated Jesus started persecuting his followers. James was killed. Peter was thrown into jail. Lydia and Priscilla were among the brave women who made up the early church. Neither of these women hesitated to spread the gospel, host the apostles when they traveled, or open their homes for meetings.

When facing challenging circumstances, many women in the Bible had friends and family members they could depend on for support. Shiphrah and Puah disobeyed Pharaoh's order together. Ruth refused to leave Naomi. Mary and Martha wept together and asked Jesus to heal their brother. Priscilla and Aquila planted churches as a husband-and-wife team.

The Christian life is not meant to be lived alone. Look for like-minded people who will strengthen you in your faith and encourage you to be brave.

And as you face situations where it's hard to speak out for Jesus, cling to God's promise in 2 Timothy 1:7: "For God has not given us a spirit of fear and timidity, but of power, love, and self-discipline." The Holy Spirit is Jesus' gift to you. His love and power will fill you with the courage to stand firm in your faith.

Pray: Ask God to bring people into your life who will help you to be brave.

Be on guard. Stand firm in the faith. Be courageous. Be strong. And do everything with love.
1 CORINTHIANS 16:13-14

Quiz Time

The New Testament women we've read about were brave and enthusiastic, and they had faith in God that saw them through difficult times. Some were friends with Jesus, and others helped start the church. Can you match each woman below with the statement that describes her?

a. Priscilla
b. Mary (Jesus' mother)
c. Lois and Eunice
d. Samaritan Woman
e. Elizabeth
f. Lydia
g. Mary Magdalene
h. Widow with Two Coins
i. Mary and Martha
j. Woman Who Touched Jesus

____ 1. These sisters watched Jesus bring their brother back to life.

____ 2. She was healed from bleeding.

____ 3. She gave birth to Jesus.

____ 4. She planted churches and shared the gospel alongside her husband.

____ 5. She gave all that she had in the Temple offering.

____ 6. These women raised Timothy to love God.

____ 7. God gave her a son after many years of waiting and praying.

____ 8. She was the first person to see Jesus after his resurrection.

____ 9. She met Jesus at a well and put her faith in him.

____ 10. She helped start the first church in Philippi.

About the Author

*K*atrina Cassel grew up in northern Indiana, lived on three different continents while her husband was in the United States Air Force, and now lives in the Florida Panhandle. She and her husband have eight children, five of whom are adopted—three from Haiti and two from the United States. They also have six grandchildren. Katrina's favorite activities are those that involve traveling and adventures that include her children and grandchildren.

Also by
Katrina Cassel

The One Year®
Devotions for Girls
Starring Women of
the Bible

The One Year®
Book of Bible
Trivia for Kids

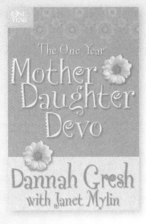
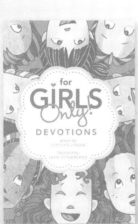

Creative projects that use your artistic talents to worship God!

60 Worship-through-Art Devotions for Girls

made to CREATE with all my heart and soul

for girls who like to draw, splotch, imagine, explore, PAINT, smudge, COLOR, think artistically, cut, get messy, tape, sketch, use your hands, use your mind, glue, spatter, write, and bring ideas to life

written & illustrated by
Lauren Duncan

FOR ADVENTURERS

The Wormling series

Red Rock Mysteries series

FOR COMEDIANS

FOR ARTISTS

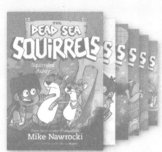

The Dead Sea Squirrels series

Made to Create with All My Heart and Soul

Be Bold

FOR ANIMAL LOVERS

Winnie the Horse Gentler series

Starlight Animal Rescue series

CP1337

MORE DEVOTIONALS — BY JOSH COOLEY —

The One Year Sports Devotions for Kids

This devotional is perfect for kids who love sports, sports trivia, and stories about athletes who overcame odds and performed the extraordinary. From the Polar Bear Club's New Year's Day swim to football to yo-yo records, the stories in this book will encourage boys and girls alike to keep reading day after day. Spiritual insight that connects the trivia to Scripture comes in the "What's the Score?" section. "On the Ball" presents a quick question or phrase to remember, and the "Coach's Comment" introduces the daily Bible verse.

Available wherever books are sold.

Heroes of the Bible

From Noah to Ruth to Hezekiah to Paul, the Bible is filled with stories of ordinary people who had heroic faith and who, through God's power, performed some pretty amazing feats! Their stories can inspire all of us to live like true heroes of faith. Get started on your heroic journey today!

Available wherever books are sold.

CP0964

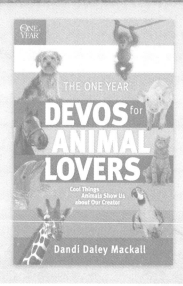

EARLY READER CHAPTER BOOKS (6- TO 10-YEAR-OLDS)

Backyard ∩ Horses

Dandi Daley Mackall

author of the bestselling Winnie the Horse Gentler series

Horse Dreams

PERFECT FOR 8- TO 12-YEAR-OLDS

CP0713

PERFECT FOR 10- TO 14-YEAR-OLDS

Join twelve-year-old Winnie Willis and her friends—
both human and animal—on their adventures through
paddock and pasture as they learn about caring for
others, trusting God, and growing up.

Collect all eight Winnie the Horse Gentler books.
Or get the complete collection with the Barn Boxed Set!